Women can return to work

In the same series:

Women can achieve career success
by Maggie Steel and Zita Thornton

The woman's guide to starting your own business by Deborah Fowler

Women can return to work

Maggie Steel and Zita Thornton

GRAPEVINE

First published 1988

Cover illustration: Photography, Richard Winslade; co-ordination and styling, Sally Rowat; checked and striped co-ordinates, Jaeger; pigskin briefcase, Mulberry.

Cartoons by Willow.

British Library Cataloguing in Publication Data

Steel, Maggie
Women can return to work.
1. Great Britain. Women. Employment — For working mothers
I. Title II. Thornton, Zita
331.4′0941

ISBN 0 7225 16428

Grapevine is an imprint of the Thorsons Publishing Group, Wellingborough, Northamptonshire, NN8 2RQ, England.

Printed in Great Britain by B L & U Printing Limited, Wellingborough

10 9 8 7 6 5 4 3 2

Contents

Introduction

This book has been written especially for you if you want to return to work or are thinking about working for yourself. If you have been at home caring for a young family or have had a career break for any reason, you are probably feeling out of touch with the world of paid work and unsure of how to re-enter the job market. What have you got to offer? Are your skills out of date? How can you sell yourself? You may even like the idea of being your own boss, especially after managing yourself for a period of time, and therefore have considered running your own business.

Career breaks can lead to a loss of confidence and direction so this book is designed to help you look positively at what you have to offer and how you can build on your past and present experience to achieve what you want for yourself.

Women *can* find success for themselves by careful planning and organization. In the following pages you will find ideas on how to get started and how to plan your route without neglecting your home and family. Each section presents a range of ideas on what you can do next and how to do it, with names of useful books and contacts to help you to take action.

Throughout the book you will find charts and questionnaires to help you get organized. In addition you should keep a file which is labelled with your name and 'Career Action File' to show you mean business. All your research and contacts should be added to this file so that you can follow your progress and see how much you are achieving.

Now is the time to start and remember, women can! Good luck.

1 Be keen to succeed

YOU MAY NEED CHALLENGE OR TO PROVE YOURSELF....

Success starts with knowing what you want. You may not have a clear idea yet but you should be able to identify some of the aspects of your needs. You want to return to work. Would you like to work for yourself? Offer a service? Develop a new skill? Change career direction? Enter public life? Make lots of money? Become famous? It doesn't matter what as long as you can say positively, 'This is what I want.' You will find out for yourself later whether you are being practical.

If you are not sure about what you want but still have the feeling you must do something, give yourself time to read other chapters in this book and follow up some of the references. Be prepared to work on the exercises and do plenty of additional research which should include making contacts and reading newspapers, magazines and journals. What you want is your destination and if you are to set a clear course there without going round in circles you must be clear what it is to be.

Why do you want it?

There are all kinds of reasons for wanting something for yourself, apart from the obvious ones like money, independence and an interest of your own. It may be a very personal reason like the need for a challenge, or to prove yourself. It may be quite materialistic like a desire to wear good clothes or to afford an expensive holiday. It could be a practical and very basic need if you are the breadwinner and have dependants. These needs form the basis of your motivation, which is essential to achieve what you want.

Motivation is a vital element in doing well, making you work hard to get what you want. It is the driving force that gives you the energy and will to persevere; it gives you purpose and the enthusiasm to enjoy the challenge you have set yourself.

One of the most common forms of motivation for women is the need to have some financial independence. Very few women are happy to rely on a partner for all their income and an increasing number of women rely on themselves entirely for income, either because they have no partner or their partner has been made redundant or has a long-term illness.

Yet motivation can stem from many other factors and one of the most important ones for today's woman is self-fulfilment. Being a housewife and mother is rarely the full-time and lifelong career it was once thought to be, with smaller families and a host of labour-saving devices to make life easier. Increasingly, women are looking for wider horizons and recognizing that they have enormous potential to contribute to society in a broader sense, perhaps even to make some changes. Autonomy, independence and challenge are now high on the list of priorities for women who don't wish to change their role as wife or mother, but add to it.

What motivates you?

One way to gain some insight into what motivates you is to look at what has motivated you in the past. When have you worked hard before to get what you want? Think of the times when you have put in extra effort and enthusiasm. Was it to prove something to yourself or someone else? Was it to gain something or to impress someone?

After four months of doing the washing up in a restaurant kitchen, Jean was promoted to waitressing with better pay and conditions. Unfortunately the manager did not like her and after two weeks trial she was demoted and went back again to the kitchen. He told her she was lucky, he usually sacked waitresses who didn't make the grade. She said goodbye and walked out – down to the town and into a large restaurant, determined to prove him wrong.

Jean became a good waitress, earning a decent wage with tips and was delighted one evening to serve the previous manager and his wife as they sheepishly ordered their meal.

Of course this incident could just as easily have had the opposite effect on Joan and destroyed her confidence – it is not what happens to you that matters so much as how you react to it. In this case a very negative incident was turned to a positive outcome.

Recognize your achievements

In discovering what has motivated you in the past you may also realize your past achievements. A useful way to do this is to draw a life line (see life line chart). Take a large sheet of paper and draw a line vertically down the centre. This is your life line. The top is when you were born and the bottom of this line is you today. Down this line you can mark in your major achievements in life, including exam passes, prizes, jobs gained or done successfully – in fact anything that you feel could be said to be 'well done'. The aim of the life line is to highlight the times when you have made progress in the past. Make sure you use a long enough sheet of paper because you will probably find one memory leads to another. Things you had forgotten will come flooding back; you have done more than you think and this all adds up to experience.

On the right-hand side of your life line write in the things you have gained or learned from each event marked. You can add comments about whether you were happy or felt confident — these will help with your personal assessment. If some of the events caused difficulties or problems write these on the left-hand side of your line. These may be times of frustration when you felt held back or your progress was blocked. What did you learn from these? Did any of these experiences change your course or prevent you from getting something you wanted? Looking back, could you have coped in a different way and brought about a different outcome? It is helpful to ask these questions because your answer may influence what you choose to do today and how you approach it.

When you have highlighted the main events in your life, both positive and negative, you may find it interesting to reshape your life line according to the ups and downs it involves. The faster your progress the steeper your line will point upwards; no change means a horizontal line and drawbacks or disasters will cause your line to dip downwards. Remember, your life line continues into tomorrow, and you intend to aim it upwards.

Avoid loss of confidence

One of the advantages of drawing an achievement life line is that it helps remind you of what you can do.

LIFELINE EXERCISE

MINUS		PLUS
	Born 1953	
Disliked school system. Didn't do any work	Started school	In Brownies, made prefect, passed 11+
	Secondary Modern School	B streamed. 4 'O' levels
Didn't like bookkeeping. Students immature	Secretarial college	RSA shorthand (80 WPM) Typing (35 WPM)
	Left home — first job	Nice boss and environment. Dealt with queries, cataloguing. Given responsibility
Closed dept.	Redundancy	
	Got 2nd job	Marketing dept. Dealt with sales staff. Wrote business letters. Kept charts
	Moved and got married	Marriage brought security. Good for confidence
Encountered sexism. Others wouldn't deal with women	Worked for estate agent	Dealt with clients. Enjoyed negotiating, looking after office alone
Motherhood shock! Didn't like being at home all day. Felt physically low and isolated	First child born	Wrote stories for James. Discovered interest in health and nutrition
	Started college	Learned to plan time. Enjoyed study. Good results
Very hard work mentally and physically. Father ill, children young	2nd child born	Gained extra confidence
Shock of bereavement	Father died	
	Joined Women's Aid	Made new friends. Got involved in community
Feel need to get back to work, use skills, earn money	Children both at school	Did PR and fund raising. Learned to speak in public.

I FEEL THAT ALL I'M GOOD AT IS CHANGING NAPPIES....

Women often say during and after a spell of looking after young children, 'I feel all I am good at is changing nappies.' Yet caring for a home and family is usually a difficult and skilled job if you include all its aspects; doing it well can be marked as an achievement. Confidence is a state of mind and can only be gained by demonstrating to yourself what you can do successfully.

It is important to avoid loss of

confidence and self-discipline by recognizing your achievements and looking at ways to build on them. A career gap is an ideal opportunity to develop new skills and gain new experience. Being at home brings you closer to the community and to the variety of activities that take place in the local neighbourhood. It is usually possible, even with the smallest children, to get involved with a voluntary group in some capacity.

When Beth had her first baby she was new to the area and had no local friends. She heard through her local clinic that there was a new mothers' and toddlers' group being set up. Although she was not a very outgoing character, she felt she would go mad if she didn't do something to get out of the house. When she went along to the group she found it quite disorganized with very little equipment and few members. She offered to write a letter to the local paper appealing for more help and for the donation of toys. The response was good and over a period of time she felt proud of the fact that she had played an important role in making the group work, as well as making some interesting friends. She also learned that she had good organizational skills and went on to do a playleader's course once her little boy was at playschool.

Evening classes are a welcome break from household routine and many courses are now run during the day, some with creche facilities. This is the time to research new ideas by reading newspapers, journals, books, etc., to find out what is available and what qualifications may be necessary. This is also the time to make new contacts and friends who may be supportive when you are ready to move on. The more you look around and take notice at this time, the more ideas you will have about what you can do when you have the time to act. If you continue to do things outside the home during a career break then you are less likely to lose confidence and feel your CV has an enormous gap.

Your priorities

To make things work for you it is important to plan your priorities. What is essential in your daily routine and what does not really matter? On the other hand, what takes up your time and attention but could be cut down or cut out completely? Clearly you want to make time for your family, your home and yourself whilst at the same time creating time for your work plans. You must be prepared to put work time high on your list of priorities if you are going to make a success of developing your career, otherwise daily demands and routine tasks will take over at the expense of progress.

Plan your time

The only way to take full account of how you spend your time is to keep a diary and draw a time plan chart.

DOES EVERYTHING NEED TO BE IRONED?...

Make a note of everything you do over the next week in your diary, including how much time is spent on each activity. At the end of the week take a large sheet of paper and mark out the days of the week in columns. List under each day the things you did and the time each one took. It will soon become clear what is being given priority by the amount of time allocated to each activity.

Where does all your time go and how essential is it?

Obviously some priorities are fixed, especially where children are concerned, like going to school, making tea, washing and ironing. Although these can't be altered you may find you could cut down on the time spent on some of your activities. Does everything need to be ironed? Could someone else collect the children on a rota? Do you spend a lot of time chatting to friends after school has started? You may be surprised by the number of hours that can be rescued from the less important activities by having a greater awareness of where time goes.

Getting organized

Drawing a time plan chart will also highlight the amount of organization involved during your day. Do you have a routine for certain jobs or do you move from one thing to another, often forgetting to finish jobs you have started? It is very easily done if you are interrupted by a caller or remembering to get to the bank before it closes. Could you improve your organization to ensure routine jobs take a set time, say first thing in the morning, to leave your mind clear for other things during the rest of the day? The more organized you become the more you are able to achieve in a day, and organization starts with plans – deciding what is important and how much time you need to complete tasks, then sticking to your plans.

Keep to your plans

Once you have made time and space for your work plans you must resolve to keep to them. They have now reached the status of priorities and this may mean saying 'no' to other things or to people. If your friends are made aware of what you are trying to do and why, you may find them a help rather than a hindrance. If you have created working time, make sure you use it to the full and don't get side-tracked; set yourself deadlines and stick to them, you'll be surprised how businesslike it makes you feel!

2 What kind of person are you?

When you have looked at some of the things that you have achieved, you should begin to get some insight into the sort of person you are. Your personality was stamped on you from a very early age and has developed throughout your life, making you more suited to some types of work rather than others. The environment and experiences that have contributed to making you the person you are may heavily influence the surroundings in which you work well. If you are used to an outdoor life the chances are that working in an office would feel very inhibiting. If you are an outgoing and sociable person you would probably find desk research or working alone very difficult. Finding the right road to success starts with working out what would really suit you.

Your personal qualities

On the personality traits questionnaire you will find a list of personality traits that cover a wide range of personality factors. Go through the list and mark a tick against those you are confident describe you well and a cross against those that are least like you. Leave those you are not sure about because you may come back at a later stage and decide for or against them, or they may highlight areas of your personality that you would like to work on.

When you have marked your list take a separate sheet of paper and list the traits you have marked with a tick. In what way can you demonstrate, using every day experiences, the qualities you have isolated? How can you show that they are really a part of you and contribute positively to the way in which you work? Look at your life line of past achievements. How did these qualities contribute to your successes in the past? How do you think they can help you in the future?

The negative qualities are just as important in helping you to decide what is right for you. It is sometimes difficult to come to terms with characteristics we may consider to be failings, but it would be foolish to overlook them. Work can be stressful and unproductive when it requires

YOUR PERSONALITY WAS STAMPED ON YOU FROM A VERY EARLY AGE....

qualities you have to struggle to demonstrate, which is why many large companies screen new candidates with a personality test.

Better to be clear right from the start about what is right for you so you can move forward positively and with confidence.

Using your strengths

By now you should be aware of what your strengths are and what they have enabled you to achieve in the past. Whatever your strong points are, they will be your main starting point for what you would like to become. Emphasize them to yourself. How well do you use your

IT IS SOMETIMES DIFFICULT TO COME TO TERMS WITH CHARACTERISTICS WE MAY CONSIDER FAILINGS....

Personality traits questionnaire

What kind of personality are you? Put ticks against the ten words that describe you best and crosses against the ten words that are least like you.

Patient ______	Moderate ______
Assertive ______	Open-minded ______
Trusting ______	Sociable ______
Eager ______	Diplomatic ______
Decisive ______	Restless ______
Confident ______	Submissive ______
Respectful ______	Sensitive ______
Friendly ______	Conventional ______
Accurate ______	Obedient ______
Energetic ______	Cautious ______
Persistent ______	Receptive ______
Timid ______	Precise ______
Cheerful ______	Optimistic ______
Animated ______	Stubborn ______
Intellectual ______	Practical ______
Pessimistic ______	Logical ______
Imaginative ______	Creative ______
Artful ______	Outspoken ______
Independent ______	Peaceful ______
Self-effacing ______	Well-organized ______

When you have finished your listing, cover your markings and ask someone who is very close to you to choose the words they think best describe you.

personality to handle events and make things work for you? Have you cultivated these strengths and developed them through experience or are you just lucky enough to be born with special abilities?

Compensating for your weaknesses

No-one was born perfect, so be realistic about your weak points. What are they and how weak do they seem? How many of them can be changed? How many have you tried to change? If you have ticked timid, submissive and self-effacing amongst your main qualities and you are not happy with this description you may recognize a need to attend a course on self-assertion and look at ways in which you can tackle your lack of confidence. If you are not happy with the way in which you see yourself then only you can do something to change this, especially if you have a good idea of what you would like to be. The greatest weakness of all is to say you can't do something when you haven't even tried.

How do others see you?

You have a self-image which is reflected in the features you have marked on your personality profile. This image can be influenced strongly by the people around you, for better or worse. It is very interesting to show the list of personality traits to a partner or close friend and ask them to mark the traits they think best describe you. You may get quite a shock if someone identifies you as cautious and conventional if you had thought of yourself as outspoken and independent. You may be lucky and find a quality highlighted that you feel is a great compliment and acts as a confidence booster.

SKILLS MAY BE DEFINED AS ANY ACTIVITY YOU HAVE DEVELOPED WITH PROFICIENCY....

How close is the view others have of you to the self-image you have of yourself? How close is your self-image to the way you would like to be? Just as you may be surprised by the sound of your own voice on a tape recorder, you would be surprised by the variety of different ways in which acquaintances may describe you. Each person may emphasize a different aspect of you depending on the circumstance in which you usually meet. It can be quite enlightening to ask friends or colleagues to give their opinion on what job or what business they would see as most suitable for you and why.

What skills do you have?

It is important to take stock of the skills and interests you have developed during your life. Skills may be defined as any activity you have developed with proficiency, usually over a period of time. Some of them may have been forgotten, with other pressures taking over and some may no longer be applicable. Make a note of the skills you think you have such as decorating, dressmaking, bookkeeping, typing, nursing, computers, etc (see skills chart). You may also include less obvious skills like letter writing, being a good organizer or a good communicator. Don't forget to include the skills employed in running a home, budgeting and rearing children.

When you have completed a list of your skills and interests delete those that are no longer applicable. Some skills will no longer apply because your circumstances have changed a great deal and they belong to an area of work you don't wish to pursue. From your list, which skills would you like to develop and use in the future? Are there any you may have forgotten but could be useful? How do these skills fit in with what you have learned about yourself so far? Which ones could you use in the job or business you would like to work in? You will see from the chart that the home and management skills you have acquired are closer to business skills than you might think, so learn to be positive about your personality, your interests and your skills then you can move on to looking positively at your future.

Identify the skills you have

Special knowledge

Hobbies	Nutrition and health. Have read extensively on the subject
College	Psychology as main subject
Voluntary	Women's issues PR. Have learned to make good use of press and marketing information
Business	Marketing. Have worked in this area in different jobs

Communications

Business	Negotiating with clients for estate agents Information-gathering and compiling a catalogue Word processing (own processor at home)
College	Essay and report writing Survey. Got distinction for project Filing. Organized a new system Letter writing in all jobs Telephone. Dealt with clients Typing. College-trained
Voluntary	Press releases. Had several successes Public speaking. Have given many talks Co-ordinating. Organized a fund raising event. Raised £600

Domestic	Budgeting. Deal with all household accounts Time management. Combined study with running a home and family, and voluntary work

People skills

Family	Caring when family are sick Patience and tolerance when family demands are high Explaining, help with homework Compromising in rows with children and husband Listening to needs of husband and children
Voluntary work	Counselling women in distress Co-ordinating, putting people in touch with each other Negotiating, getting agreement from others Persuading, enlisting the help of others Making contact, approaching new people

Creative

Domestic	Writing. Write stories for children Sew and knit for the family Decorating. Do most of own interior work
Voluntary	Ideas. Made several useful suggestions on strategy and fund raising for Women's Aid

3 Build up your confidence

LOOK AT YOUR LIFESTYLE AND THE ROLES YOU PLAY....

Confidence is the vital key to success; when you've got it everything seems possible because you are filled with optimism. Unfortunately, too many women suffer from lack of confidence, which blocks their progress before they have even started. There is no knowing how much talent and potential is wasted by women who feel unsure about themselves and are therefore unwilling to push themselves because they fear failure or rejection. Doors are closed by phrases like: 'I don't think I could do that,' or 'I couldn't possibly cope with all this!' In most cases this is lack of confidence rather than lack of ability. Confidence says 'You could if you tried'.

Confidence can be developed but you must be prepared to work at it. It is a state of mind that can be created by turning negative thoughts into positive ones and by turning thought into action. Each action successfully completed is a building block for your confidence. Here are five areas to concentrate on:

Know yourself

What kind of person are you? You have looked at your personality characteristics and what type of person you are but what does it all mean? Look at your lifestyle and the roles you play: mother, wife, daughter, worker, provider. Put together all these things make you the person you are. Look again at your achievements; these have made you what you are. What do they all add up to? How do they contribute to your confidence? Think of the last time you felt really confident. What gave you that feeling and how did it help you? Make a list of other things that have given you confidence – a compliment from a friend, a thank-you for something done or a task achieved to your satisfaction.

Knowing yourself well provides a firm basis for deciding what is right for you and what you must do to develop your aims. If you can draw a clear picture of the person you are today; your likes and dislikes, strengths and weaknesses, personality and abilities, then you can begin to understand your needs and aspirations. Other people may have their own ideas about you and these may influence the way you feel, but what is important now is what you see in yourself. From now on you must stick to what you want by having a clear idea of your purpose.

Ask for what you want

The old saying 'you get what you ask for' is never more true than today. If you feel other people walk over you ask yourself 'Why do I lie down and let them?' What stops you standing up and saying 'this is how I feel and this is what I want'? Are you afraid of what others will say or do? How can they hurt you? What have you got to lose by stating your needs? You have a right to be considered. By asking you have everything to gain – including respect – but you must learn to be assertive.

Self-assertion training is very popular with women today, demonstrating yet again the need for women to develop more confidence. Although courses are extremely helpful, there is no reason why you shouldn't start working on your technique immediately. The aim is to influence people you deal with so that they listen to your point of view and accept your needs, whilst in return you are able to listen and accept from them.

Wendy attended classes and found them very useful in helping her to understand types of people and their behaviour without taking all their actions personally. Yet she still had the barrier of dealing with people in authority to cross. She still felt intimidated by certain people and unable to state her needs.

Wendy is a very attractive young lady with beautiful hair and is regularly in demand as a hairdressing model. She was very loyal to a particular hairdressing salon and, in return for modelling at their publicity events, she was given credits to have her hair done as a form of payment. Yet Wendy began to feel unhappy about the way she was being treated because, although she had worked for these credits, she was not treated with the same consideration or respect given to other customers. Appointments were cancelled and pressure was put on her to accept the salon's choice of hairstyle rather than her own. The credits given were not related to the value of hair treatment. A perm, tinting or a cut were given the same credit value, yet in reality a perm was worth much more than a cut. As Wendy never had perms or tinting, she felt her payment was diminished in value and that the salon was taking advantage of her.

Wendy is a gentle and amiable person and, rather than make a fuss, she preferred to go to another salon and pay for her hair to be done in the way she wanted, despite having many credits in her account. She was going to leave and perhaps find work with another salon, without explaining why and no doubt she was going to be successful. In discussion Wendy admitted she got on well with members of the salon, including the owner, but that she had never voiced her feelings so that on her last two visits she had left them feeling annoyed and frustrated. Whilst she was explaining her problem she began to see that it was partly her own fault

GO TO YOUR WARDROBE AND EXAMINE ITS CONTENTS.... HAVE YOU GOT STYLE?...

that things were going wrong. How were they to know their practices were unacceptable if she was not prepared to tell them? Wendy knew she must go back and be firm about her choice of hairstyle and remind them she was a customer and wanted to be treated as such. When the next modelling job was offered with them she would tell them the terms she felt were fair and acceptable to her. If they still didn't accept these then she would go elsewhere, but at least they would know why!

Wendy's example can be transferred to many other situations and often things go wrong because we have not been sure or clear about what we want before we enter into a situation. The lesson is simple: know yourself, what you want, and ask for it. People respond with more respect to clear but reasonable requests and you gain tremendous confidence from discovering this method.

Develop your style

It is easy to recognize style when you see it but have you got style? Look at yourself in the mirror. Are you pleased with what you see or slightly disappointed? Do you look smart or can you see the effects of putting home and family before yourself for the last few years? Has your choice of hairstyle, make-up and clothes moved with the times or are you still wearing what suited you five years ago? Looking good and feeling good is an important source of confidence and it is something you can work on now.

Start with your hair. Has your style taken account of the fact that your face is changing with age and experience? Does it do the shape of your face justice or have you been avoiding the cost of investing in a good cut? Is your hair healthy and easy to manage? Are you still bleaching or perming it yourself and does it look obvious? Your hair should match your style, short or long, straight or wavy. It should always look well groomed and healthy – there are plenty of preparations available to help you make sure it is – and it should be businesslike for working purposes. If you haven't already got one, find a good hairdresser and resolve to get advice and styling regularly.

Next your make-up. If you don't wear it perhaps now is the time to start. The older you are the more you need to consider the use of some make-up, which should enhance, not drown your features and make you look lively. It need only take a few minutes to improve your looks using a very small amount of foundation, eyeshadow, mascara, blusher and lipstick, skilfully applied. If you feel unsure about what make-up is right for you, contact one of the many home consultants to get advice. They are not too expensive and you can cut the cost by getting some friends together for a joint session. These consultants use colour coding, which is designed to look at your skin type and find the shades of make-up that are right for you. This should also influence the colours you wear in your clothes. Local colour counsellors usually advertise in the press, otherwise ask your friends if they know of anyone who sells make-up from home.

Dressing for confidence is a must. Clothes influence not just the way you feel but the way in which others see you. Go to your wardrobe and examine its contents with a cool, critical eye. Is it full of clothes you have had for some time, including some you never wear? Does it contain a wide variety of items which are difficult to match up, or does it strike you as rather dull and full of neutral colours? Be prepared to be ruthless. Take out everything you haven't worn recently and any item that has given good service and looks past its best. Try things on and remove anything that does not do you full justice because it is the wrong shape, colour, style or size. Put them all in the jumble bag and resolve to wear only what really looks good, separating casual from business wear.

Now concentrate on your business look. How many outfits can you put together, including shoes, handbags, belts, scarves and jewellery, that make you look smart? You need to have fewer items, well co-ordinated in colours that suit you and to use your accessories to create different, fashionable but fairly classic looks. Make a list of essential items that may be missing to complete an outfit: a belt, a blouse or a pair of matching shoes. Stick to buying only what you need from your list, even in the sales, where impulse buying is a great temptation. If your wardrobe doesn't contain a good suit or jacket start saving now; you can't fail to impress in a suit and your confidence will be given an enormous boost by feeling smart and businesslike.

Plan your success

We have already talked about the importance of planning to make good use of time and to sort out what is important to you. Planning is also a very useful way to give you confidence in taking steps to achieve your aims. If you have followed the exercises so far you know where you are at present and what has brought you to this point, but where would you like to be in five years' time? If you know where you are going in the long term you will develop a purpose in what you are doing because you will begin to concentrate on activities that help you move in the right direction. Even planning on a daily basis gives a greater sense of confidence because you are clear about what you need to accomplish that day and you will gain satisfaction from being able to see what you have achieved.

Believe in yourself

Confidence is a state of mind that starts with believing in yourself and knowing you can do anything you really set your mind to. It is an attitude that refuses to allow you to be put off by fear of making mistakes or worrying about what other people think. Keep an open mind when you listen to others and accept their views and suggestions without feeling they know better. Trust your instincts and follow them because they are much more likely to be right for you than other people's ideas. If you can do this you will begin to feel in control of your circumstances and will be able to use the power this gives you to move in any direction you choose. Whenever negative thoughts start to take over, make a conscious effort to switch them to positive. Your mind can only concentrate on one thing at a time so make it something good. Everyone has a reserve of inner strength so make yours work daily to build up your confidence by believing in what you can do.

4 Planning the next step

Every step you take forward is a continuation in some way of things you have thought of or done in the past. Ideas which have formed in the back of your mind are almost certainly the result of past experiences and the knowledge you have gained about yourself. Your circumstances and personality are a major influence on your achievements whether by choice or not. The aim now is to identify where you are and to make sure that you exercise greater control over your destiny.

Where are you now?

In Chapter 1 you have looked at your past achievements by drawing a life line, and in Chapter 2 you examined your personal qualities. Both of the exercises have been designed to help you gain an objective view of the type of person you are and of the qualities and skills that you possess. They will also help you focus on long term goals, giving you ideas about which direction to go in the future.

Your ambitions

If you were asked to write a description of where you would like to be in five years' time, what would you say? Back in a full-time job? Running a small business? Using a professional qualification in some capacity? You may have other ambitions — like retiring to a sunny place or running a campaign to change something in your community.

Fix your ambition clearly in your mind because it represents your goal for the future. You may have more than one idea. That's fine. Make a note of them on paper to go into your personal file.

Whatever your ambition may be, it is important to recognize right from the start that there will be hurdles along the way. Take Linda, who was accepted as a law student, travelling from a London suburb into the centre of town every day. It was very hard going as the mother of two young children, and costly with no grant and expensive books to buy. Then at Christmas Linda's father tragically died, shattering the family and creating many extra responsibilities. It was too difficult for her to continue studying under the circumstances. Sensibly, Linda discussed her problems with her tutor and will take a break until she is able to resume her full-time course. In the meantime she has taken a local part-time job to help with the cost.

Going back to study is hard work and usually means unsociable hours, especially at exam time. Any small business requires money to invest and lots of hard work with very little return in the early days. Finding a job and selling yourself can cause problems if you have had a career break or lack sufficient experience. Plans help you sort out what can be achieved and what is going to lead to disappointment without further action. Set your goal at a level which remains in sight because it can always be reviewed as you make progress and gain confidence and experience.

Determination

Whatever your goal, your starting point must be a strong determination to succeed. Determination means having a clear idea of what you want and the perseverance to see it through. With determination you will be prepared to reach your objectives despite the problems that will inevitably occur. When difficulties arise you will meet them face to face and find the necessary solutions to overcome them. You will learn that real confidence comes from the power to find answers and get round problems. Armed with this skill you will find your own success.

Setting objectives

Objectives are the staging posts leading to your goal. They describe what you must achieve before you can reach your goal. They are measurements of time and effort, marking the steps forward. Look at your five year plan. What changes or developments must take place to reach your vision?

Kay works as a part-time, unqualified teacher in a nursery school but feels she would like to gain a proper qualification and develop a full-time career. Her vision of herself in five years' time is not crystal clear because, although she enjoys her job, she also loves making quilts and has a good eye for colour. Her vision has three strands:

- she can take a degree in English and do research work or teach
- she can seek a qualification in

design and look to developing a career as a consultant in interior design

- she can develop her quilting talents into a small business selling to private customers or exclusive shops.

Although the ideas Kay has may seem very diverse, the starting point for them all is to do some research. Her initial objective must be to find out as much as possible about courses and career opportunities for her first two aims and see what is available in her area.

She is married with two young children so this will have to be taken into account when deciding what is feasible. She must also look seriously at what opportunities there may be to convert her hobby into a business and gain some idea of whether it is likely to be profitable. The very act of looking, asking questions and accumulating information will help Kay to eliminate some ideas and develop others.

Action plans

Much of the planning so far has been done on paper with the knowledge that they can easily be changed. The next stage of planning is much closer to home because it determines what you must do now to make things happen. Action plans are a list of those things you can easily identify as necessary steps to reaching your objectives. They are drawn up on a short time scale with a deadline ranging from a week to a month depending on your circumstances. They don't need to be in any special order but you do need to set a date for completion. Kay's action plans may include:

- going to the library and checking through career sections
- obtaining prospectuses from local polytechnics and colleges
- contacting careers advisory services
- phoning any acquaintance who knows about design consultancy
- making an appointment with an enterprise agency.

Each item should be timetabled into Kay's schedule for the next four weeks.

One of the nicest things about having a list of things to do is the pleasure of crossing off items as they are completed. The information you gain as you work through the list should be collected in your file and sorted into appropriate headings. At the end of the month you can take a good look at what you have learned so far and where it leads to. This will help you develop your ideas and form the basis of your next set of action plans. Each set of completed action plans brings you a stage closer to your objective and helps you realize more clearly what you can achieve.

Making progress

Using this formula you will find great satisfaction in knowing you are making things happen. You are no longer wavering or dreaming about what you may want to do; you are now doing things. It cannot be stressed enough that action in this way will bring its own rewards by adding to your pool of knowledge and opening up possibilities. You are being productive and, if your plans are realistic, you will find what you are looking for.

The importance of making contacts

A very high proportion of business is conducted by using contacts. By nature most of us prefer to deal with people who are known to us. The art of developing contacts is simply a matter of keeping a contact book — a list of the names, addresses and phone numbers of all the people you know, and identifying those who may be able to help in some way. Make your list as long as possible. Go through your address book. Think of people you meet at the school gates or knew in previous jobs. Think of friends' husbands or friends of friends — you'll be surprised at how long the list can grow.

Women often show a great reluctance to operate in this way, feeling it may not be well received or it is not the 'done thing'. In fact it is an extremely enterprising approach that can bring rich rewards. Usually people are flattered when you ask them for help or advice and are very willing to help you on your way, being both interested and supportive in what you are doing.

Getting started

When you have made a list, put a star beside the names of people you feel confident will be most helpful. Choose just one of the names, telephone them and chat about what they are doing and what you hope to do.

Making contact in this way can often be mutually beneficial. You may have some useful information to offer in return. At the same time you establish your position; you are moving on and this will be remembered for future reference by your contact.

Using networks

There have always been informal networks in operation from the traditional 'old boys' network' to various self-help groups, but the number has grown tremendously, particularly in recent years. Networks are lines of communication created and maintained for the purposes of making contacts. They are usually centred around certain types of businesses or occupations. For example, City Women's Network was created for professional women to keep in touch, while the Women's Video and TV Network was started to encourage women to go into the film-making industry. Other networks are built around particular interests, like the Women's Register or the National Childbirth Trust.

Many networks were designed to be self-help groups seeking to deal with problems which often isolate individuals, like Cry-sis, a support group for parents with babies who cry excessively, or the Asthma Society for the growing number of people who suffer from this condition. The important aspect of using a formal network is that it gives you instant access to many contacts in a chosen area as well as useful information. The advantage of joining a formal network is that it can fill the gaps in your personal network and they are usually geared to encourage self-help, offering access to expertise. Lists of women's networks are available through the Women's National Commission (see the useful addresses at the back).

Create your own luck

How often do you hear people explain their own or others' success in terms of luck? True, luck is a great asset on the road to success just as bad luck can set you back many paces. Luck very rarely appears as a bolt out of the blue. It is much more likely to be the result of chances you have created by your own actions. By doing things, making yourself known, taking an interest in what is going on around you, you are creating opportunity. Luck comes from being prepared to recognize and meet opportunity where and when it arises. It is the response to what is possible and lucky people are more often those who have developed the ability to spot the chances and turn them to advantage. You too can create your own luck!

Paying attention to appearance

Now that you are well on the road to making progress in your life, it is a good idea to take a look at yourself in the mirror. Is the image reflected anything like the vision you have of yourself in the future? Do you look good or are you still wearing what suited you five years ago? When did you last buy some make-up, change your hairstyle or sort out your wardrobe? Taking a lively interest in your appearance is a sign that you care about yourself. If you have doubts, go to your wardrobe immediately and look at what is available. Do you have enough choice to look different as well as smart every day of this week? If not, throw out what is past its best and plan what you will need to make improvements.

If you refer back to Chapter 3 you'll see that you can build up your confidence by projecting your image and developing your style. Top businesswomen all agree that it is essential to be smart and stylish, and that clothes can be a powerful reflection of authority, competency, capability and confidence. Your appearance must reflect this self-confidence in the type of outfit you wear, your make-up and your hairstyle.

Facing up to the problems

Going back to work can be difficult. It is very easy to use obstacles as an excuse for not bothering. Here are some of the problems and possible solutions. Remember, the most important thing is to take a positive view; most problems are not insoluble.

'I haven't got time to work and look after my family'

If you have read thoroughly the rules for time management in Chapter 1, you will realize that a working mother can have enough time for home, husband and the family and often the time that she can give is better. How many mothers at home all day find themselves washing up, feeding the dog and answering questions about life and the universe all at the same time? You can follow the time plan, allowing time specifically for individuals in the family without feeling guilty and this will benefit the whole household.

A set time each day spent getting involved with the children, playing, painting or reading stories, will be appreciated far more than using the whole day just looking after them. Choose a job that fits in with your lifestyle and which allows you some time to spend with your family. Avoid jobs that require you to work a large amount of overtime and try not to bring work home. Make sure that there is some time in the week when you and your husband will be at home together. You will be surprised at how much you enjoy his company and at how much he appreciates yours after a day spent in a different environment.

Don't worry if the time you choose to spend with the family is at the expense of housework. Men and children are usually not too worried about everything being in its place. Don't let it bother you. However, if a tidy house is a high priority, then consider paying someone to help with the housework. It is a tonic to arrive home at the end of a working day to find the house looking cleaner than when you left.

'Who will look after the children?'

This is perhaps the biggest problem working mothers face. There is a sad lack of child care facilities in many areas. However, they do exist and there are several options open to you. You might consider hiring a nanny. If this seems expensive try sharing a nanny, or employing an au pair who could solve housework problems too. If you don't have the space or would regret the lack of privacy then consider nursery schools or a childminder. The Working Mothers Association produce a handy booklet detailing child care possibilities and where to find them. They also provide support and advice for working mothers.

Paying someone to look after your child can be expensive and it is easy to think that financially it is not worth working. Hopefully by the time you have read this book you will be aware of the other benefits of going back to work. You will definitely end up with some extra money — enough to provide a holiday or a new dress that you would otherwise not be able to afford.

'Will my children suffer?'

It is quite common to feel guilty about abandoning the children to be looked after by someone else. This is, in fact, quite unreasonable. Children have to be allowed to

THE CHILD WHO HAS ALREADY STARTED ON THE ROAD TO INDEPENDENCE, ADJUSTS TO SCHOOL MORE EASILY....

become independent. It happens anyway when they start school and it is a good idea to let go of the reins gradually before then. Many primary school teachers say that the child who has already started on the road to independence adjusts to school more easily than those who come straight from spending every day with their mother. They are usually more confident and more able to mix with other children. You probably already take a small child to a toddler group for these reasons. Often the child will not worry about whether you are there or not. You may also spend time visiting friends, chatting while the children play, and paying them little attention. In fact, the step to child care is often greater for the mother than the child.

The important thing is to make the right choice of child care – one that both you and the child is happy with. You must, above all, trust and like the carer. If you feel that you can't send your child to a stranger then consider asking friends or family or a combination of them both. So long as the arrangement is regular your child should fit into a routine quite happily. You may not know any friends who are childminders but you'd be surprised at the people who respond given the suggestion that they try it. The advantages are that both you and your child know her and she possibly has children about the same age attending the same school. If you can't find a friend to oblige, try putting a notice up at the school gate with your requirements. Perhaps a person you don't actually know but who you exchange smiles with might be interested. By using a childminder you will also be creating a job for someone else, someone who is at the same stage as you – wanting to return to work.

'What if my arrangements break down?'

There are times when the best child care arrangements fail. The carer, her children or your children may fall ill or other arrangements might have to be made during the holidays. It is wise to have temporary back-up solutions for times like these. Family, friends and neighbours are usually very helpful in an emergency. If illness is causing the breakdown of arrangements the time that extra help is needed is likely to be quite short. Friends will probably be willing to look after your children for a day or keep them for an hour after school, but you will have to have the courage to ask a few of them to cover the whole period of illness. Make it clear that you are available to reciprocate the favour if ever they need help. You should at least be able to reduce the time absent from work to a minimum.

If your own child is ill the only alternative may be for you or your partner to stay at home and look after him. Illness is unavoidable in yourself and your child and as long as it doesn't happen constantly employers tend to be understanding. There is no doubt that having to find emergency cover is a headache but the times when your child care arrangements fail will be very few over the whole year. Holidays can cause problems to people with school-age children who have managed to find a job to coincide with normal school hours. Holiday playschemes are available and leaflets giving details are available from libraries. The times, however, may not fit in with your working schedule but they may help with part of the day. Again, you may have to ask friends or neighbours to take or collect the children from these schemes. Perhaps the teenage child of a neighbour might welcome the chance to earn some pocket money.

If you work part-time, consider child-sharing with a friend. You look after her child while she works and she looks after yours while you work. Although this sounds quite hectic it works particularly well during the long summer holiday when children become bored and wish to play with friends anyway, and when the weather may be good enough to spend lots of time outside.

For short holidays and half term you may have to take work home if possible, use some of your annual leave or take the children to stay with relatives.

'Even if I work from home, will my children lose out?'

One way of avoiding problems with child care is to take on work at home. More is said about this later but many of the worries concerning home and family are very common to all working mothers, whether they work at home or not. Pat was faced with these problems when she decided to write a book for parents of sleepless, crying babies. She had spent years at home when her children were small, involved with Cry-sis, a voluntary organization which gives support to such parents.

'Writing the book – something I had never done before – required self-discipline (especially having two young children at home – then five and two years old). It often necessitated working in the evening when the children were in bed, at weekends, or at spare moments when the children were out playing with other kids, or even when the children were around but playing happily at home. I would sneak off into the kitchen or the study to do a bit more until finally they wanted me or something came up. I tried to see the book as a side-line to the kids — otherwise it is easy to resent their demands and ignore them for the sake of getting on with the book.

Inevitably, I felt guilty. Was I spending enough time with them? (I am not one to spend all my time with the children anyway, and am a strong advocate of them playing amongst themselves, which has paid dividends in confident children who are sociable and good in groups.) And then at times I felt guilty about the amount of time I spent with my husband. I often escaped to the study, doing a bit more when a TV programme came on I didn't like much. But I think he accepted that, and I struggled with the fine balance of being around but working whenever possible.

It is hard working at home when you have small children. It is difficult to get the balance right. There will always be people who suggest that you are doing too much; taking on too much; not spending enough time with the family; pursuing selfish motives; all these things. You have to be resolute and sensible. You have to become a master at snatching a few minutes here and there and making use of spare time — not to do unnecessary housework or to perhaps join in coffee mornings with friends but to get on with work as and when the opportunity presents itself. You have to be able to concentrate hard for short moments, to tune in quickly, to get on without supervision, to stop automatically when something else comes up.

The book seems to have been a success. It is very gratifying. Lots of people have said "Well done".'

It is easy to be concerned about the rest of the family and forget oneself. Going out to work can bring its own personal rewards and the family soon adapt to new situations like that of you not being there all the time!

'There is no part-time work available'

Many people feel that they can only cope with part-time work while their children are small but complain that they can't find it. In fact there is part-time work around but it is concentrated in a few occupations. It is neccssary, therefore, to have an open mind about the sort or work you wish to do and even of side-stepping from your ultimate career goal and trying something different.

Most local institutions, hospitals, schools, colleges and local councils have part-time posts as do many shops, restaurants, manufacturers and banks, so these are a good place to start. Anyone seeking part-time work has to have initiative as these jobs are so in demand that they are not always advertised. Ask friends already in part-time jobs to tell you of vacancies that arise. Make personal enquiries to the personnel department of these places. Read the books that are available which detail types and locations of part-time work. They may give you ideas that you had not considered before. Be prepared to try something different.

If you really feel that you do not want to change your profession or deviate from you career plan then consider going into something related. For instance, there is little part-time work in teaching so consider adult education or literacy schemes. Chapter 8 discusses the advantages of part-time work in terms of career development and gives ideas on how to create part-time work through different work patterns such as job sharing.

'I've no real experience'

This is often what mothers are led to believe by prospective employers at interviews. Remind them about the skills involved in running a house and family. Every mother has to control some sort of budget even if it is not entered formally into account books. She also has to plan ahead thinking about shopping for the week's meals or remembering when the muddy football kit needs to be used again. She will have had years of clock-watching in order to organize her children's timetable of leisure pursuits and get them to school on time. Some mothers have to organize their lives around their children's different levels of education — school, part-time nursery and toddler groups.

If you still think that this is a problem for you, turn back to the skills and life line exercises you

REMIND THEM ABOUT THE SKILLS INVOLVED IN RUNNING A HOUSE AND FAMILY....

carried out earlier and apply for jobs with the confidence of these behind you. Don't forget to include all the voluntary work you may have done while being 'just a housewife'!

5 Bridging the career gap

Having a break from work means that you have the time and energy to grasp new opportunities and follow new ideas. It is a time to gain experience, develop skills and make new contacts and friends. It provides the space to try things out or catch up on education. Doing some of these things will help you to avoid loss of confidence and mean that you are achieving something whilst at home.

There is no reason why anyone used to following a busy work routine should feel that once at home they will become insular, lonely and cut off from real life. A career break can be considered as a positive asset.

Find time for friends – old and new

It is wise to remain involved with past interests and keep in touch with friends. You now have the time to visit people and listen to different points of view. You may find it easier to become involved in new interests with a friend than alone or to join new groups and meet new people. If you have to go alone don't assume that everyone there is very confident; they may be waiting for you to approach them. If you meet people whom you like and get on well with don't be shy to encourage the friendship by inviting them round for coffee. Keep in contact with working friends too as they will keep you in touch with the world of work.

It is important to balance your life so that it is not all concerned with home and family. While it is a good

THERE IS NO REASON WHY ANYONE SHOULD FEEL THAT ONCE AT HOME THEY WILL BECOME INSULAR, LONELY AND CUT OFF FROM REAL LIFE....

idea to join groups such as the National Childbirth Trust who will provide advice and support, it is also wise to attend talks and discussions revolving around other subjects, such as those run by the Women's Register, the Women's Institute and your local women's group. These will provide a way to achieve balance.

Get involved

Make an effort to attend groups regularly and become involved with your local community. Try joining mothers' and toddlers' groups, a community association, drama or singing groups, parents' associations or commit yourself to education (see Chapter 9 for the full range of training ideas). If you are concerned with local issues join a campaigning group. You can read more about these in Chapter 12.

The time may come when you wish to take part in the running of a group. Don't feel that you will be pressurized into doing this; the choice will be entirely yours. If, however, you would like to become more involved, do offer your services, even if the group is not advertising for help. No voluntary organization will refuse another pair of hands and you will be able to give as much time and commitment as you choose.

Pat became involved with a voluntary organization in its initial stages when her first child was ten months old.

'This took a fair amount of time – giving talks, writing articles, preparing information on the group and so on. It was convenient to fit in around family life. If there were difficulties at home, the voluntary work could take second place. It was, I considered, a commitment so I always tried to meet deadlines and treated it as a "job". My husband was a little resentful that I spent time and effort, not to mention money, on something which was not bringing in financial rewards. However, I saw it as a worthwhile interest. It gave me something interesting and exacting to do; it was a challenge. It brought me in touch with the media; I had articles published, met interesting and authoritative people.'

Where to find organizations

To find out what is on offer locally look for posters in the library, ask at the Citizens Advice Bureau or join groups already attended by friends. Events organized by local groups will be publicized in the local paper where

THINK ABOUT THINGS THAT YOU HAVE A SPECIAL INTEREST IN....

you will often find requests for help from groups. Details of church-run groups such as Young Wives can be obtained from that church – you don't have to be of that faith to join in. Church halls often hold mothers' and toddlers' groups; your health visitor should be able to direct you.

Church halls and community centres are sometimes the venue for sports and leisure clubs and amateur dramatic groups. Again these are usually advertised on the premises. Sports centres and swimming pools usually support sporting clubs. Think about things that you have a special interest in, for instance birdwatching or walking and develop this interest in the company of others by joining a local branch of a suitable group such as the Royal Society for the Protection of Birds. You can obtain local branch details from the National Headquarters, listed in the phone book, or look in the diary column of your local paper.

Many people offer their help to a voluntary organization, based on experiences they have had or through special interest in a particular field. You can contact the National Council for Voluntary Organizations for a list of the headquarters of various organizations who will tell you if there is a group locally. If you are less sure about the type of voluntary work you want to do then contact your local volunteer bureau or 'helpline'.

Jill had been involved with voluntary work in a small way when she applied for a college course to train to teach mentally handicapped children and found that she had nine months to spare before it started. She became a community service volunteer working full-time at a Women's Aid centre. When college started she became a welfare officer attached to the students' union and she also helped out at local nurseries and playgroups. Before she was able to teach however, she found herself mother of twins.

'Suffering from severe post-natal depression, with two babies, one of whom slept for one hour and cried 23 hours a day, I had no energy, saw very few adults and was miserable. By the time the twins were eight months old, I was beginning to regain some of my confidence but not enough to apply for real jobs. I had by then become involved with the Association for Parents of Sleepless Children but only on a very ad hoc *basis. I decided that what was needed where I lived was a mothers' and toddlers' group and I contacted some like-minded mums by putting a notice up in newsagents' windows. We set one up. Dead easy – badgered the vicar for use of the hall, put a few posters up, persuaded people to come and I think it is still going.'*

Jill then joined a women's network organized by a monthly magazine.

'For me at the time it was a life saver. I was able to go out and meet real people with a title and an organization backing me up. When you feel low it is much easier to say "I'm Jill from ..." rather than trying to sell yourself. For that reason I would advise anyone needing experience to go for a recognized organization. The best place to start

is with the Council for Voluntary Service for your area or, if it is a rural place, the rural community council. Both of these, if they don't have a voluntary bureau of their own, will know the best place to go.

If women do feel they want to do some voluntary work there are certain do's and don'ts:

- *do be reliable*
- *don't overcommit yourself – two hours a week of enjoyed time is better than six of time you can't manage*
- *be honest about what you want (if you are offered something you can't stand the thought of say so or you'll end up doing something you don't like and leaving with your confidence shattered).*

BE HONEST ABOUT WHAT YOU WANT.... OR YOU'LL END UP DOING SOMETHING YOU DON'T LIKE....

Lots of places that do voluntary work will also offer training – take it if you can, as it all helps.'

As a result of her experience working with voluntary groups Jill got a job-share working with self-help groups. Then another job came along, working for Save the Children at a centre for parents, organizing courses and weekends away, giving talks, listening to people and running groups.

The value of offering your service

It might seem as though voluntary work is a way of giving a lot but gaining a little in career terms. In fact such work is very valuable for the future. Through it you have the chance to gain work experience. You are likely to have opportunities that you would never get in paid employment. You will be able to show a future employer that you have drive and initiative and can work as a responsible part of a team. It is possible that you will have shown that you possess organizational and managerial skills. You will probably have worked in several different areas and may identify an area you had not previously thought of working in.

Sue sums it all up saying:

'The benefits are enormous in the end. You have done something which requires you to discipline yourself during time at home. You have kept in touch with the outside world of work. You have found a niche for yourself and discovered skills you may not have realized you ever had. You have learned to work with others as equals – not an easy task for someone used to being either the underdog or the top dog. You have achieved something – however little – worthy of self-praise. Your confidence is greatly improved, your skills not allowed to go rusty. You have had a campaign to strive for, a purpose and a challenge. All of this and much more, makes you a better person in the end. That apart, you are also working for something very worthwhile, whatever it is. People are being helped and that reflects on your own character and makes you stronger and more capable.'

Voluntary work, as you saw from Jill's experiences, can often lead on to a different type of career when you are ready to return to work. Social services and hospitals appreciate prospective employees who have had similar experience in the voluntary sector. There are some services, such as the probation service, the Citizens Advice Bureau and Marriage Guidance Council, that offer training to people who volunteer to help.

Changing direction

Pat's experience in voluntary work also led on to other jobs. She wrote a book for parents of crying, sleepless babies and was then offered part-time work on a research project on crying babies. She is also hoping to promote a TV series about mothers' experiences with new babies. Eventually she hopes to start a business enterprise using the talents she has developed whilst being at home.

Pat used the new interests and skills she had developed to make a change of direction. Having a career break is a good time to consider this. There are many reasons why you may feel that you would benefit from doing so. It could be that you never felt entirely happy in your previous career; maybe you made a wrong choice early on. Perhaps you always felt that you were still searching for the right thing to do. There could be practical reasons why a change of career is necessary, for instance, if you had the type of job that is not compatible with having a family. Maybe the work involved long hours or it was necessary to bring lots of work home to get through it all. It is possible that your job took you away from home for periods of time. When you are also doing the job of housewife and mother it would be difficult to return to a job that involved any of these things.

It could also be that like Pat you have realized that you have skills that will lead you up a different avenue and would like to utilize them in your career. We have said that undertaking education is a good way of bridging the career gap and you may find that you want to gain more qualifications with a specific career goal in mind. This is a good time for retraining and updating your knowledge. There are some careers which you will not be able to return to without doing so as basic things will have changed while you have been away, for instance a career involved with law in any way. There are also new careers such as computing for which training was not available when you were at school.

How to find out what career qualities are necessary

If you do decide to change direction you need to find out what skills and qualifications are being asked for today in those jobs. One way of doing this is to write to companies in that field and ask them. This has the added advantage that when you are ready to enter such a field you can write again and remind them of your previous interest and the help they gave you. Alternatively, if you have a contact in the type of area in which you wish to work, gather your courage, phone them and ask for a few minutes of their time to discuss ways in which you could break into this type of work. Otherwise you should be willing to phone cold and ask to speak to someone in a similar job to the one you would like to have.

You can also read books giving career advice – even if they are aimed at school leavers. In some ways starting again is just like starting for the first time. Careers advisory centres deal mainly with school leavers but they are the people with the most up-to-date careers information.

Read the recruitment adverts in newspapers or trade journals. These will not only give you details of the qualifications sought but also the qualities needed for the job. You may also find ideas for jobs you hadn't considered before.

Another reason for a change of career may be that when you were first deciding, there were certain jobs that women just didn't do. These jobs are now opening up to women, with many employers keen to show there is no sex discrimination in their

company. It is no longer unusual to see women engineers, lorry drivers and pilots, and there are actually special training courses designed to encourage women to enter these professions, which you can find out about from your local job centre. In fact with the latest technology there are very few jobs women can't do. Look around at features in magazine articles on women who work in 'a man's world' and read how they have been accepted and made a career for themselves.

One further reason for starting again is that you may have been dissatisfied with a service you have experienced and feel that you could do better. You may have experienced the frustration of trying to get follow-up service from a large company where getting through to the switchboard is the first hurdle. You have then got to find the right person to deal with your problem and then get someone to call at the right time to repair the fault. How often have you found sales assistants abrupt or unable to answer simple questions about the product you are interested in purchasing? These experiences may give you ideas on how services can be improved and if you feel you would enjoy working in any of these areas you may use your ideas to sell yourself to a possible employer. Follow all the previous advice for information on how to become a trainee in that field, or consider setting up your own service. Chapter 10 gives advice on working for yourself. If you would like to compete against bad service, it may be the perfect opening for a new business.

It is not always necessary to start all over again when considering a

THERE ARE VERY FEW JOBS WOMEN CAN'T DO....

change of direction, especially if you already have good experience or qualifications. You may even feel that your experiences while taking a career break will enable you to return higher up the career ladder than your position when you left it. In these cases you can contact a career consultancy for advice such as those run by Women in Management or PER (Professional and Executive Recruitment). You may find you are advised to accept a lower starting point than you would choose in order to prove your abilities and gain promotion. Women who have been prepared to do this often find they can catch up quite rapidly if they work at it.

You can also use your time at home to gain work experience in different fields by doing part time work or trying different working patterns. This is discussed more fully in Chapter 8 but remember, when it comes to going back to work and selling yourself, it is skills and experience that come top of the list for most employers so it is worth the time and effort spent on bridging the career gap.

6 Finding a job

By now you will have reviewed your skills and interests, or possibly undertaken some training and you can use the 'ideal job' questionnaire to gain a better idea of the type of job you would like. As we have said before, it is important to remain flexible in your choice and see how some of your skills fit into the job market. There may be jobs that you see advertised that you have ignored because you are not familiar with their title. It is a good idea to talk to friends and acquaintances about their job and other jobs in their field and also to look through the careers books in libraries so that you are aware of the possibilities.

SEE HOW SOME OF YOUR SKILLS FIT INTO THE JOB MARKET....

You may like to contact the National Advisory Centre on Careers for Women who, as well as offering a career counselling service, have a careers publications list. If you have a degree or a higher qualification you can enrol with the Professional and Executive Recruitment Service at your local job centre who offer a free newspaper and advice for posts at managerial level.

Make a job of job hunting

Having considered all these things, decided on the working pattern and child care that you would prefer, you will be ready to find work. You should make a job of job hunting and work to the best of your ability. Try to be enthusiastic and organized. Don't tackle it in a half-hearted way. Follow all the avenues for finding a job and apply for several at once. Keep good records of the jobs you have applied for with copies of your application form and covering letters kept in files for easy reference – you will need them to refer back to and to improve your technique.

Your ideal job

To clarify your ideas about what sort of job you'd enjoy and be suited to, tick the appropriate boxes below.

Type of employment

- Retailing ☐
- Manufacturing ☐
- Services ☐
- Professional ☐
- Other ☐

Working pattern

- Full-time ☐
- Part-time ☐
- Job sharing ☐
- Freelance ☐

Locality

- Local area ☐
- Nearest town ☐
- Commuting to city ☐
- Travelling ☐

Working environment

- Own office/at home ☐
- Small office ☐
- Open plan ☐
- Factory space ☐
- Shop floor ☐
- Outdoors ☐
- Other ☐

Working team

- Alone ☐
- With boss ☐
- With partners ☐
- Small team ☐
- Large group ☐
- Other ☐

Responsibilities

- Keeping up with a team ☐
- Working alone with a particular task ☐
- Assisting another person ☐
- Co-ordinating or supervising a team ☐
- Managing a project ☐
- Setting up a system ☐
- Dealing with customers ☐
- Giving a caring service ☐
- Checking/recording details ☐
- Other ☐

Skills used

- Communication ☐
- Decision making ☐
- Administration ☐
- Teaching ☐
- Problem solving ☐
- Caring ☐
- Creative ☐
- Artistic ☐
- Handiwork ☐
- Other ☐

Be prepared for rejections

It is most likely that you will receive rejections from some of them so it is best to be prepared for this and put them down to experience. Don't take it personally; nearly everyone who has applied for jobs has experienced rejections and the sensible ones take the chance to learn from it. It may not be that you are lacking in skills or experience; finding a job is also a matter of luck, of being in the right place at the right time. The opinion of one employer is not always that of another, so although you will be disappointed, don't let your confidence be sapped. If time goes on and you still have not been successful, don't panic, you will eventually be lucky.

Check your job hunting method

If your job applications are not achieving much success perhaps you should reconsider your curriculum vitae and covering letters. Maybe you are not selling yourself well enough. Take advice from friends, family or career consultants. Maybe you are not applying for the right jobs. Perhaps you should reconsider your choice. If you have opened a job hunting file and kept copies of all your letters as well as those received from employers, you may find the reason why you have not been successful. Think of the interviews you have attended and the questions you were asked. Were there any clues as to why you may have been rejected?

The cost of finding a job

Apart from the cost of your ego, job hunting can be an expensive business by the time you have paid for your travelling expenses to agencies and interviews. Phone calls, stamps, papers and journals soon add up so try to save on some of these things by using a 'job club' if there is one at your local job centre. These aim to give advice and facilities for job applications if cost is a problem. Read newspapers and journals at the library rather than buying them all.

When applying for a job you will have to consider locality. Although ideally you might prefer only to work in your local area it would be unwise

to restrict yourself too much. It is often as easy to travel several miles by a good public transport system in to the nearest big town than rely on poor provincial services. Don't forget to take the cost and time needed for travelling into account. It will certainly be more expensive to travel in to a large centre and may, because of the extra time, involve greater child care costs, although sometimes this is offset by larger salaries and wider opportunities.

When considering part-time jobs,

add on the travelling time to the working time and be quite sure that the hours fit in with you. You may find that you will gain a great deal more from working full-time than from a part-time job which takes up most of every day. With part-time work particularly it is important to think carefully about locality and hours.

Where to look

The first place to go is your job centre where you can get advice on registering as unemployed and on whether you are eligible for any benefits. It is important to do this as some jobs, such as community programmes, require its applicants to be in receipt of benefit for a qualifying period. Here you will find advertised local jobs, both full- and part-time. Anyone can walk in and browse amongst the cards displayed advertising jobs. If you find one that interests you write down the number and approach one of the staff; they will usually ring the employer to arrange an interview or tell you how to get an application form. You can also spend some time with a member of staff detailing what you are looking for and build up a relationship so that they can contact you if something suitable comes in.

Visit all the job centres in and around your area on a regular basis. Don't forget to ask for details of the Professional and Executive Recruitment service mentioned earlier to receive your copy of *Executive Post* which includes job adverts as well as articles on career development.

Read the newspapers

Jobs of all types are advertised in the situations vacant columns of newspapers. Most areas have a number of local papers including at least one free issue which, while being a good source of local jobs, also includes jobs available in neighbouring counties and in the nearest town. You should therefore start looking through these as soon as they are issued. Here you will find local education and health authorities advertising as well as companies, small businesses and even individuals such as a doctor requiring a receptionist or a mother requiring someone to help with domestic duties. Try to read the adverts in the local papers of neighbouring areas as well, particularly if they constitute a different borough.

In order to look for a job advertised in a national newspaper it is necessary to be more selective. The type of job advertised will on the whole reflect the type of reader that the paper attracts. Thus a paper like the *Sun* and the *Daily Mirror* will include vacancies in skilled and semi-skilled jobs as well as those for the forces, the police and the fire or ambulance service. Advertisements for professional management and executive jobs will appear in papers such as the *Telegraph* or the *Guardian*. These will also offer jobs of a similar type on the same day each week, so once you know what you are looking for it should only be necessary to read a specific paper once a week. However, jobs advertised in national papers have many more applicants and you will have to apply immediately. It is therefore wise to form a routine of visiting the library to look at these papers on the day the adverts that interest you appear.

The other type of journal that you must include in your job search is the specialist trade press. These usually appear on the same day each week. Some are available in the library but you will have to subscribe to the more specialist ones. There should be a directory of trade publications available in your library, detailing where to obtain copies. Remember that these journals also offer jobs in related fields or those requiring similar skills, so that you will not only find teaching jobs in *The Times Educational Supplement* and the *Guardian*, but also jobs requiring organizational skills such as co-ordinators for national charities. All of these newspapers advertise jobs throughout Britain, and sometimes even overseas, but most of them will be with companies which are based in London or south east England. It is important, therefore, that you keep looking in your local paper so that you don't miss jobs in your area.

How to read the advertisements

There are many different types of advertisements and so it is useful to be aware of what the various sizes and styles imply. All are governed by cost, from the large full- or half-page type, through the 3 cm boxed, to the one- or two-liner. These don't reflect how keen the business is to recruit staff but how large their recruitment budget is. The size of the advert will therefore give you an idea of the size of the company. Current advertising costs in a national daily paper can be from £8 per line to £58 for a column centimetre displayed in a box.

Reading a job advert is rather like buying a house or choosing a holiday – you have to be able to assess what is really meant by the advertisement.

> **Start now**
>
> Come and sell in the leisure industry. High commission paid weekly. Full training given if you are new to selling. A south coast location of quality.
>
> Telephone (046) 38 292 and ask for Bill.

An advert such as this one in fact tells you very little. Obviously it is for a salesperson, but selling what? Anything from books to exercise cycles! How? By telephone, door-to-door, party plan? And where? The south coast is a large area. If you are interested in selling I don't suggest that you ignore this advert but that you ask and expect satisfactory answers to questions such as these.

> **A millionaire at 50!**
>
> We can't promise that but we can offer a terrific part-time job. You need a car and spare time on Friday evenings and all day Saturday.
>
> Ring Mr Brown on (094) 46 382.

Despite its gimmicks all that this advert tells you is when you would be required to work! As it was found in a local paper and has a local phone number you have a rough idea of where it might be, too.

You will find other similarly vague advertisements, varying in size, appearing in the national newspapers and requiring applications from 'ex-company directors', or 'graduates' or to 'join the professionals', or if you have 'a record of achievement' for careers in investment, marketing or commerce, etc. The best adverts will have the name of the employers; be quite specific as to what the job entails; mention salary, holiday entitlement and qualifications required. Beware of any organization that expects you to work on commission alone or invest some of your own money, if it is a good business this shouldn't be necessary.

Many advertisements carry a telephone number and it is a good idea to ring up armed with any questions concerning things that you are not clear about. This will give you a chance to chat informally to the recruitment officer and you may refer to this conversation later in your covering letter with your application form.

Newspaper advertisements need not be your sole means of finding a job – you can also join an employment agency. This will cost you nothing as it is the employer who pays. Although some agencies cover a variety of jobs, others are very specific to one trade, such as nursing or domestic staff. Look in the yellow pages for listings of those near to you.

Some agencies work a preliminary vetting service for their employers so it is best to go prepared as you would for an interview and in some cases you may be required to take a test. If you are considering temporary work you will probably have to approach an agency.

Hidden job vacancies

Despite all these avenues, the vast majority of jobs are not advertised externally at all. For this reason you need to let everyone, particularly those already in a job, know that you are looking for work and ask them to keep an eye on vacancy boards or tell you when a vacancy is likely to arise. You will then have to write a letter asking to be considered for the vacancy. You will find details of how to do this in the next chapter.

7 Selling yourself

When it comes to actually applying for a job first impressions are all-important. If you don't sell yourself well at the first opportunity you will not have a second chance. You and the people who know you may realize that you are perfect for the job, but you have to convince an employer who doesn't know you at all and only has your application to go by. You should by now be well aware of your skills and capabilities. Now is the time to sell these assets and in order to do that well you must believe in them yourself.

Your Curriculum Vitae

Your personal advertisement for your assets is your *curriculum vitae*, usually known as the CV. It is the story of your life on not more than two sides of paper! Your CV will be read by a busy recruitment officer who will also have to read many others so it must be short, informative and neat, in an easy-to-read format. From this, judgements will be made about you and your suitability for the job.

Presentation

Your CV should be typed with no mistakes on good quality, white, unlined paper. You can find office services who will type your CV through local newspapers. The layout is important and usually as follows:

- name
- address and telephone number
- date of birth
- marital status
- education and qualifications
- work experience
- additional skills

CURRICULUM VITAE

Name: Felicity Sparks	Address: 24A High Street Oswestry Shropshire
Date of birth: 6/9/50	
Age: 37	Tel: Oswestry 7244
Marital status: single	

EDUCATION AND QUALIFICATIONS

1961 - 1968		Holy Trinity secondary modern school
	O levels	Maths, art
	CSEs	English language (grade 1), English literature (grade 1), domestic science, French
1968 - 1969		Shrewsbury College of Further Education
		Shorthand and typing RSA stage II

PREVIOUS EMPLOYMENT

1982 to the present	I left my last job as personal assistant before the birth of my son and have spent the last five years as a full-time mother and household manager. Having to manage on a tight budget has taught me a great deal about financial planning.
1983 - 1986	Childminding.
1977 - 1982	Personal assistant to the head of a department of Smithson building works. Responsible for correspondence, supervising the office junior, shorthand and typing.
1975 - 1977	Clerical assistant in the wages department of Smithson building works. Duties included typing, filing, ordering stock.
1971 - 1975	Clerk/typist with the Inland Revenue. Responsibilities included typing, filing, organizing the staff work rota.
1969 - 1971	Office junior at the Lancaster Building Society.

INTERESTS

I am involved with the parents' association of my son's school (St Mary's) and hold the post of secretary. I also help with publicity for social events.

REFEREES

Mr D. Hart
Head of finance
Smithson building works
Ferry Lane
Shrewsbury

Mr W. Gallagher
Headmaster
St Mary's School
Royal Avenue
Oswestry

CURRICULUM VITAE

Name: Joanne Broadwater	Address: 27 Alfred Street Bassenthwaite Cumbria
Date of birth: 22/8/58	
Age: 30	Tel: Bassenthwaite 574
Marital status: married	

EDUCATION AND QUALIFICATIONS

1967 - 1973	Keswick High School
July 1971 O levels	Biology (B), Chemistry (B), Maths (C), English Language (C), English Literature (D), French (C), Geography (C)
July 1973 A levels	Biology (C), Chemistry (C), Maths (D)
1973 - 1976	Carlyle Polytechnic
	B.Sc. 2.2 in agricultural sciences

WORK EXPERIENCE

1976 - 1981	Research assistant, Plantwell Seeds Ltd.
From 1981 to the present	While taking a career break to bring up two small children I have been following an Open University postgraduate course in agricultural sciences in order to ensure that my knowledge and skills are kept up to date. I have one credit left to gain an M.Sc.

INTERESTS AND ACTIVITIES

I enjoy outdoor leisure pursuits such as rambling and regularly organize rambles for our local group.

I have spent some summer holidays as a volunteer leader on an environmental holiday project for children.

OTHER INFORMATION

I hold a driving licence and have been trained to drive a minibus.

REFEREES

Mr George Sutton
Head of plant breeding
Plantwell Seeds
King's Lane
Keswick

Mrs Irene Fallon
Course Tutor (summer school)
27 Mill Lane
Workington
Cumbria

- activities and interests
- names of referees.

Your CV should not be more than two pages long and each page should be typed on only one side (see sample CVs). You should leave spaces between each section and the headings should be underlined. Under these headings should be included everything that will highlight your skills and achievements. Education should go back to 'O' levels, if you have them, and include any qualifications gained since. These will be easier to read listed down the page rather than in a continuous run across the page. In-service training courses would be better listed under the relevant section of work experience unless they resulted in a formal qualification. Work experience should also include unpaid work which should be noted as carefully as details of a paid job. It is usual to start with your most recent experience and work backwards.

Try to avoid gaps giving explanations for any career breaks if possible. Never give negative facts; your CV must be a positive statement. A mature candidate once listed under the heading qualifications: 'none'. If he really had none it would have been better to leave out that heading completely but in fact he had attended various training schemes which he was advised to list.

An example of a poorly written CV

Although a handwritten CV may be acceptable it would be better typed.

When dealing with work experience you need to give dates, position held and the name of the company, and it is here that you really have to sell yourself. This is no time for false modesty. Write a brief description of what your job entailed, any responsibilities you had and any successes or new ideas that you introduced. If you had many different jobs, limit your list to the last five to ten years or explain job-hopping by a desire to gain experience.

In 'additional skills' you should consider anything that might be useful, such as the ability to drive or speak a foreign language or type to a reasonable standard. If you have none, again leave this out.

Leisure interests should be mentioned briefly as they give background information to your total image and may provide a talking point at the interview.

LEISURE INTERESTS GIVE BACKGROUND INFORMATION TO YOUR TOTAL IMAGE....

The age is better written out even if the date of birth is included. It saves the employer working it out.

Marital status is missing.

These details are not necessary.

Name: Jasmine Lewis
Address: 22, The Grove
Coventry
Warwickshire

Date of birth: 21.4.62
Height: 5'4"
Eyes: Blue
Hair: Fair

Education

These would be better listed down the page as in a table.

'O' level, June 1978: Music (A) English language (B) English literature (B) French (C) Maths (C) Biology (C) Geography (D)

'A' levels, June 1980: Music (A) English (B)

September 1980 – July 1981

First year of a teacher training course at Dudley College of Education.

It would be better to give the reason for leaving especially as she went into full-time employment following successful holiday jobs with the company.

Previous employment

Cover short holiday jobs with one general statement.

April 1979 – September 1980

Saturday girl at Benetts department store

August 1980

Worked full time at Benetts department store (one month)

Give details of job position held.

Try not to split categories when using more than one page.

Avoid spelling or typing errors.

Unexplained gap from 1984 to the present day.

(Previous employment contd.)
November and December 1980

Coventry sorting office - Christmas post delivery

1981 - 1984

Assistant to the buyer, Benetts Department Store

<u>Interests/activities</u>

Music
Part of the Coventry Choral Society. Play the organ at my local church. Acheived music exams grade IV. While at college, played 2nd flute in the orchestra. Sing in a rock band in the evenings.

Sport
Sailing, swimming, aerobics, squash, waterskiing.

<u>Travelling</u>

1978 Went backpacking around Europe (6 weeks)

1979 Toured North Africa (1 month)

1980 Spain, Italy

1981 Sailing holiday in Greece

These would be better written as a list as it's easy to skip over details and miss things when written across the page.

This gives the impression that there will be little time left for working. Try to achieve a balance between having varied interests and too many demands on your time.

Holidays need not be listed. Perhaps include travelling under the list of interests and expand at interview.

Do not run on to three pages.

Give details of position held and any training undertaken if any.

Always write out abbreviations in full.

Who is this person? State job title.

Don't give relatives as referees.

Voluntary work

1985 - 87 NCT

Additional skills

Driving licence

Referees

Miss Tuson
Benetts Department Store
High Street
Coventry

Mr D Lewis
49 Crossway
Coventry
Warwickshire

The covering letter

Whereas your CV can be photocopied to use for various job applications, any accompanying letter will pinpoint the most relevant aspects of your CV to the job (see sample letters). It should be short, to the point, and preferably handwritten on good quality, unlined paper. Above all it should be neat. It should reflect your keenness, reliability, flexibility and determination to succeed. Address it, if possible, to the person handling the recruitment. You could find their name by ringing up the switchboard of the business concerned. It should then start, for instance: 'Dear Mrs Searle' and end with 'Yours sincerely'. If you can't make it personal then start 'Dear Sir/Madam' and end 'Yours faithfully'.

Start the letter by mentioning the post applied for and where you saw it advertised. Pick out the most relevant qualifications and experience you have and point out how your skills make you suitable for that particular job. You might like to give reasons why you would like to work for that particular company and, of course, why the job appeals to you and why you think you would be so good for the job. You have to convince the employer that you are the best candidate. The point of this letter and the CV are to interest the employer enough to want to meet you at an interview. Your CV and letter should be posted in a large envelope and you can ring to ensure that it arrived safely; CVs have been known to get lost or end up in the wrong department.

Speculative applications

You will also have to sell yourself on paper when making a speculative application. Many jobs are never advertised and this letter is to find vacancies before they are advertised so that you alone are considered. Companies are usually happy to receive these because it can save a lot of time, money and effort to recruit without having to advertise. Letters can be sent to many companies on the off-chance that a vacancy is about to arise or even that a post might be created for you (if you are very convincing!). A letter of this kind shows initiative, interest and determination and should be accompanied by your CV. The first paragraph could include a reason for approaching that particular organization; consider size, reputation or new areas of expansion. As in your covering letter, relevant parts of your CV should be brought to the

2 Standard Avenue
Enfield
Middlesex
8th December, 1987

Mrs S. Brown
LTW Group PLC
Company House
4 Elena Road
London N2

Dear Mrs Brown,

With reference to my recent application to you for the position of personnel officer, I would like to thank you for your letter explaining that at the time you had no vacancies.

You did, however, expect vacancies to be coming up in the immediate future and as it is now some weeks since that time, I wonder if you could give me any more definite information on your progress in this matter. As I said in my original application, I am keen, hardworking and determined to succeed in an industry such as yours. I can assure you of my continued wish to join LTW and to contribute to its growth if given the opportunity.

Yours sincerely,

Kathy Richmond

Karen Rosen
33 Mays Avenue
Cardiff
12th February, 1988

Mrs S. Lewis
Women's health group
St Mark's Hospital
Royal Avenue
Cardiff

Dear Mrs Lewis,

One of your colleagues, Jackie Howard, has mentioned to me the possibility of there being opportunities within your group for enthusiastic people keen to enter this area of the health service.

I am very interested in developing a career concerned with women's welfare and would like to make a long-term commitment to training and working in this field.

As you will see from my CV, I have had nursing experience and the temporary nursing jobs that I have taken on from time to time over the last two years have enabled me to gain experience in different aspects of nursing.

If you do have any vacancies in the near future, I would appreciate the chance to speak to you in interview at your convenience.

I look forward to hearing from you.

Yours sincerely,

Karen Rosen.

27 Ferny Hill
Croydon
Surrey CR60 3PL

29th April 1988

Mr P. Strachan
Disabled Venture Project
3, Forest Road
Croydon
Surrey CR16 1RU

Dear Mr Strachan,

With reference to your advertisement in the 'Evening Echo' on Wednesday 28th April, I would like to be considered for the post of group organizer.

As you can see from my CV, I have had some experience of working with disabled children on a voluntary basis, which has involved day-to-day care as well as administration and fundraising, and has allowed me to develop an understanding of the problems encountered by these children. It has also given me valuable grounding in dealing with people in general.

If at all possible, I would appreciate the chance to visit Holloway House to meet the staff and children, and learn more about the project.

I hope you find my details and objectives interesting.

Yours sincerely,

Linda Penton

LINDA PENTON (Mrs)

attention of the employer and the same rules of selling yourself apply. A third paragraph could include your aims and objectives and the letter might end with a sentence similar to this:

'Although I appreciate that you may not have any opportunities in this area at present, I hope that an informal interview can be arranged to discuss possible openings in the future.'

The interview

Most people find this a nerve-racking experience. It helps to remember that to arrive at this stage means that you have already made a good impression. You, along with many others, may well have received previous rejections, so to reach this point of your job application shows a certain level of success.

Be prepared

The interview is not to put you on trial; it is to try and find out if you are suitable for the job and likewise it is for you to see if the job is what *you* want – don't forget that! In order to avoid panic you can do a certain amount of preparation. This will help you feel more confident at the interview.

If you receive an interview date by post, phone the company to confirm that this is suitable for you. You should also speak to an assistant in the personnel department or to the secretary of your interviewer so that you can find out the following:

- the name(s) of your interviewer(s) and their position(s) in the company
- the full job description for the post (it is essential that you have some idea in advance of what your responsibilities would be)
- whether there are any written details about the company that may be available, such as promotional brochures, sales leaflets, etc
- that you have been given the full details of where you are to be interviewed so that you don't go to the wrong building
- how long the interview is likely to take (this will allow you to make provision for the children to be collected if necessary and will also give you an indication of whether you are likely to be tested in any way)
- whether the company is willing to pay travel expenses (some companies only pay second

interview travel expenses, but in any event it is worth asking what their policy is on this *before the interview*).

This information will give you a clearer idea of what the employer is looking for and will help you avoid making unnecessary mistakes on the day. You can then go on to make more specific preparations, for example:

- gather as much additional information about the company as you can by going to the library to look at trade directories or the EXTEL cards which are kept on microfilm. Ask friends or relatives who may have had contact with the company; make sure you know about its size, functions and locations
- compare the job description with your personality profile, achievements and skills lists and think of the ways in which you feel you match the requirements of the job. Prepare some concrete examples of how you demonstrate the qualities they are asking for; for example, if the job requires a good eye for detail think of a hobby or tasks you have done that would demonstrate this ability
- check your travel arrangements thoroughly and give yourself plenty of time to arrive early and allow for traffic jams or train delays. It is said that one in five applicants arrives late for their interview. This gives a bad impression. If necessary, make a trial run to anticipate the difficulties that might arise
- check your wardrobe and your interview outfit to make sure it is clean and pressed and that you have matching accessories to give a smart impression. Interviewers are said to make their decision in the first few minutes so appearance counts a lot
- run through some of the questions you are bound to be asked like 'Why do you want this job?' Use your family to rehearse giving answers, asking them to behave like an interviewer.

The point of contact

It helps to arrive at the interview in time to go to the ladies' room to repair your hair and make-up as well as to compose yourself. Everyone is nervous when attending a job interview so try not to be put off by those feelings of panic if you suffer from them. If you have done your homework and look your best then you should look forward to the opportunity to talk about yourself;

let's face it, most people do!

The moment you walk through the door of the interview room you will be making an impression so try to remember the following points:

- if you have a coat or umbrella it is best to leave it outside the actual interview room
- when you meet your interviewer smile and say 'good morning' or 'good afternoon'
- walk forward confidently and give a firm handshake
- sit well back in your chair with your hands relaxed in your lap

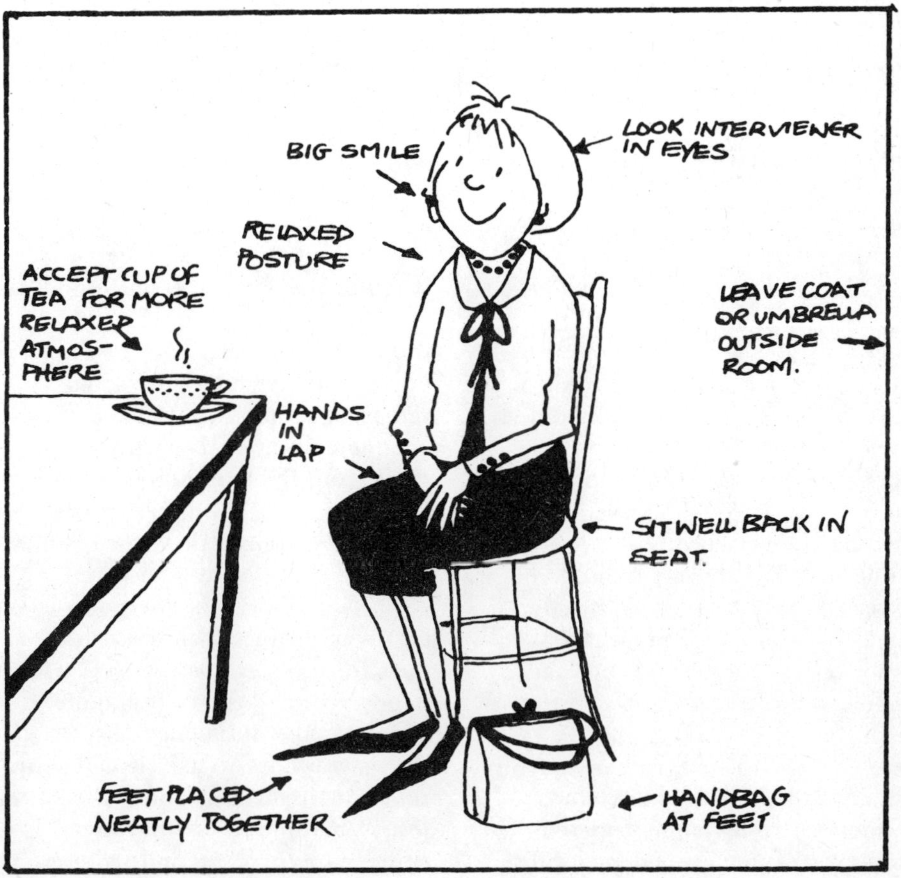

- place your bag at your feet rather than holding it in front of you like a shield

- don't smoke but do accept tea or coffee if offered, to create an informal atmosphere.

If you are faced with a panel of interviewers don't be put off. Try to remember which position each person holds and then you can tailor your answers to suit the questioner. All interviewers are different, some well prepared, some not, some very formal and others extremely informal. Most interviews start with small chat to help break the ice and give each side a chance to size the other up.

Although it is impossible to have anticipated and rehearsed all the questions you will most likely be asked, you should be prepared for the most obvious ones like 'Why did you leave your last job?' or 'Have you done this kind of work before?' Use your answers to sell yourself, so don't give quick one-word replies. Avoid being negative about anything you are asked, even if the answer strictly speaking is 'no'. There are always other related facts you bring out to enable you to respond to questions with 'yes' which invites the interviewer to listen, rather than 'no', which is likely to lose his interest. Remember to use some concrete examples of your experience skills based on your preparation.

Listen carefully to each question and think before replying. Answer in a polite, calm and positive way, being as honest as you can. Don't try and avoid difficult questions because this will be noticed with suspicion. If you have prepared your homework well you should have worked out answers to problem areas in advance. Whatever difficulties you have had with previous jobs or in your personal life, leave them behind you; no interviewer wants to know about problems you may present with 'personality clashes' or 'not agreeing with your previous boss.'

You may be asked questions about how you will manage the journey to work, if you live a distance away, or whether you have adequate child care arrangements or even whether you think a woman can do the job. Don't be upset by seemingly personal remarks, simply try to give an adequate and positive reply. Look for signs from the interviewer of whether you are talking too much (a common problem) or too little, which is not going to sell you to the company.

As said before, the interview is a two-way process; you must ask questions to see if in fact you will be happy working there. It is quite in order to take out a check-list of things you need to ask; it will show that you are serious about taking the job. Why did the vacancy arise? Is the company expanding and will the job expand too? Find out about your working hours, salary, holidays, pension schemes, health insurance or other benefits.

Some employers are prepared to assist with travel, and some offer interest free loans for bus and train passes, so ask about this:

You should also find out your exact responsibilities, to whom you will be responsible and the opportunities for promotion. Ask questions about the products and services of the company; it will help demonstrate your interest and enthusiasm. Ask also about training opportunities they may offer you as an employee; it will show that you mean to learn and improve on the job. If you run out of questions tell the interviewer they have been very helpful and covered all the aspects you wanted to know about. The last question you need to ask before leaving the room is when the result of the interview will be known.

After the interview

Hopefully you will have convinced the employer that you are the best person for the job. If, however, you haven't heard anything after a week ring up and ask if a decision has been made. If you have been rejected see if you can find out why. It is probably that there was a more qualified or experienced candidate amongst the other applicants. Sometimes you may be given a reason that will help you to prepare better for the next application. Remember that on average a person has to attend 10 interviews before getting a job. Don't be too disheartened at a rejection and never let it affect your enthusiasm for further job hunting or affect the way that you approach the next interview, other than to improve your technique. Put each interview down to experience, then forget it and start afresh.

8 How to fit in work

Time Savers

Some activities eat up your time unnecessarily. Below are some of the ways in which you might be able to save time:

- cut down on the time you spend on the phone
- learn to say 'no' when too many demands are being made on you
- set a definite time for routine tasks
- buy weekly from supermarkets if you can. Get groceries delivered if you can't, as well as newspapers and milk
- video favourite TV programmes for a more convenient time
- reserve time for reading papers and magazines for when you are too tired for anything else
- organize a rota for daily trips to school or playgroup.

After a career break for whatever reason, you may not feel ready or able to jump straight in to full-time work. You might still have home and family commitments, small children or an elderly parent to care for. You may wonder how on earth you could possibly fit in work with all your other day-to-day responsibilities. However, it is possible to cut down on some of the activities which eat up your time unnecessarily. You can analyse how you spend your day by filling in the time plan chart and by re-arranging and delegating some of the time-consuming routine tasks included in the list of time savers. On the other hand you might not feel confident enough that you will be able to cope with work or you may want to try something different. If this is the case it is a good idea to slide into work gently by considering a different working pattern.

Part-time work

The advantages of part-time work are, on the one hand, obvious: the

Time plan chart

Use the time plan chart to work out how you spend time in a typical week or personalize your own version of this and write down everything you do from getting up to going to bed.

	7–9 am	9–11 am	11am – 1 pm	1–3 pm	3–5 pm	5–7 pm	7–9 pm	9–11 pm
Monday								
Tuesday								
Wednesday								
Thursday								
Friday								
Saturday								
Sunday								

ability to fit work in with your lifestyle or to maintain a regular income while starting a business, and on the other hand less obvious: it forms a chance to increase your confidence and gain experience, increasing your chances of gaining full-time employment when it suits you. It offers the chance of variety by combining two part-time jobs in different or related fields.

Cathy had not had a permanent job for five years. She recently went to an interview for a Saturday job.

'I was rather nervous, as it was my first interview for a number of years, and the interviewer made me feel worse. She kept going back to the fact that I hadn't worked for five years and questioned whether I would be able to cope and if my husband and children would manage without me on Saturdays. I felt a total lack of confidence at the finish.

I had thought about doing childminding for some time but wasn't sure about looking after the children of a complete stranger.'

She then saw a poster placed by someone she knew at the school gates requesting a part-time childminder and took up the opportunity. After a while a vacancy for a school meals supervisor at the school was advertised and Cathy was a successful applicant!

'I think childminding might have helped me go to the interview in the right frame of mind, so giving me more confidence. If I had not had the experience of looking after other children for a length of time, I may have doubted if I was capable.'

As it is, Cathy now has two part-time jobs that fit in well with her children's school hours and some experience of working with children which will help her eventually when thinking of a career. In fact many part-time jobs (such as those already mentioned) and playgroup leaders, school crossing patrols, etc., are particularly suited to mothers at home with children.

Other part-time work can take place during unsocial hours – at weekends or during the evenings – particularly those concentrated with the manufacturing or retailing industries. To some, however, this can be an advantage as it is possible to work when your partner is at home with the children so not having to make child care arrangements.

The greatest disadvantage of part-time work is low pay, low status and loss of benefits. Most people therefore see it as a temporary arrangement, the first step to full-time work. It has been said that there is a lack of availability of part-time work. In fact there is quite a lot around but it is concentrated in a few occupations. This, however, may be

ONE IN 25 WOMEN DOING CLEANING AND CATERING WORK HAS A TEACHING QUALIFICATION....

an advantage. There is a value in side-stepping from your ultimate career goal and trying something different. You may return to your goal or you may decide to change direction. A TUC report, *Women in the labour market*, published in 1983, reported that one in 25 women doing cleaning and catering work has a teaching qualification, one in 12 a nursing qualification and one in six a clerical or commercial qualification.

Linda joined the Queen Alexander Royal Army Nursing Corps as a student nurse but gave it all up 15 months later to marry a guardsman. Her husband's career in the army was more important than hers and the two of them, and later her son, were often on the move. When her son had started school and with her husband often away for long periods of time, she began to feel bored on her own all day long. At first she tried evening classes: 'A' levels and pottery, then voluntary work as a teacher's aide. Eventually she was paid for this position and began to consider doing part-time work. She became a school meals supervisor for four hours a day. Then they were posted back to England:

'It hit me! What am I trained for? Nothing.'

Her local job centre suggested a course in secretarial skills, sponsored by the Manpower Services Commission.

'Armed with my diploma I applied for a full-time job at a building society.'

But before she was able to take up the position they were given notice of another posting, this time in the north.

Linda decided that, in view of her lifestyle, she would stick to part-time jobs. She worked for a while in a boutique doing everything from window dressing to banking the takings. She worked as an administrator in a hospital for the mentally handicapped. She took a job in a pub/restaurant serving at tables and ended up cooking. She was gaining different experiences: 'I thoroughly enjoyed it — well below my capabilities and the money was negligible but it was great fun.'

Eventually her husband left the army to join the police force.

'Suddenly it dawned on me, no more months away from home for Kev. In fact shift work meant that he would be home for all or part of the day. Therefore I didn't have to worry about Shaun at all and maybe I could think about getting a decent permanent job.'

Linda decided on clerical work and despite being told: 'No previous experience and over 25 — employers will see you as a harassed housewife!' She applied for several jobs, both full- and part-time and took a part-time position with the Inland Revenue. Six months later she applied for and got a full-time post. However, she was no longer working alongside other part-timers, mothers like herself, but found herself with highly qualified youngsters in her team. This could be quite daunting to someone just starting work again but Linda had enough experience to have confidence in herself.

'It took quite a bit of getting used to. The first three months were quite unhappy but I just concentrated on learning the job and doing it well. A lot of the younger ones seemed to moan about the job but I was just glad of the opportunity to start something new and it showed. My report read: "Her keen enthusiasm is refreshing".'

She gained promotion in the face of competition and is now well embarked on her new career.

On course, with some professions it is possible to return on a part-time basis or to a related area of work. For instance, teachers could consider supply teaching, private tutoring or adult education. The Manpower Services Commission sponsor a series of books with ideas for different working options. Published by the Careers and Occupational Information Centre the titles include: *What else can a housewife do? What can a teacher do except teach? What else can a secretary do? What can a nurse do?*

Job sharing

There may be no part-time work in your field or you might not wish to change direction or drop to the bottom of your career structure. If this is so you will have to consider creating part-time work by job sharing. This differs from part-time work in that it consists of two people sharing one full-time job, dividing all the benefits such as holidays, between them. Job sharing opens up opportunities for people who do not wish to work full-time and don't want their career prospects to be affected or who want to combine a career with other interests. One reason why friends or even couples job-share is to share the care of small children.

Although job sharing has been successful for a number of years in other countries, interest in this country has been slow. However, there has been an enormous growth of interest in recent years and this type of working is now widely accepted. The way that a job is shared in terms of hours and areas of responsibility depends very much on the needs of the job itself and the partners. This is a very flexible way of working.

What kind of job can be shared?

It is possible to share almost any job at any level, even managerial positions. The most important thing to consider is the person with whom

IT IS POSSIBLE TO SHARE ALMOST ANY JOB AT ANY LEVEL....

you are likely to share work. There has to be good communication between partners and you have to have the same ideals. You don't, however, need the same skills – it is a positive advantage in a job share situation to have complementary but differing skills. Job sharing also has the advantage that you form a team and provide support for each other. New ideas can be discussed and developed between you both.

How to find a job-share

Many jobs are now advertised for sharing, particularly in local council, many education authorities and banks. You can also contact a job sharing project that operates a job-share register. To find out if there is a local group in your area contact New Ways to Work. They will also give you support and advice on all aspects of job sharing and can keep you up to date with the job sharing situation nationally. They have a number of useful publications, either free or for a small fee, concerning everything from where and how to find work to how to negotiate a contract for job sharing.

Perhaps you have a friend, maybe someone already doing part-time work, who would share a full-time job with you. Look through your contacts or people in your workplace if you already undertake part-time work and suggest forming a team. Once you have a partner you can then apply for full-time positions, even if they are not advertised as a job-share. You will, of course, have to convince employers of the advantages; the fact that he will be getting two for the price of one; that he will get a greater spread of skills and manpower at busy times and will have continuity for 52 weeks of the year, as holidays will be taken at different times. New Ways to Work can give you further ideas on how to convince a new employer. Remember, though, to retain your job security by working out what will happen if one of you leaves. Will you be happy for your partner's position to be advertised?

If you cannot persuade anyone to partner you, advertise in professional journals or local newspapers and pass the word around that you are looking for someone to share a job with. Alternatively, apply for a full-time job alone and see if the employer has any suggestions for a partner.

Temping

Temping or casual work provides a means of working that need not be regular. You will usually be filling in for someone who is absent. This could range from a single day to a few months. You will be able to work whenever it suits you. This pattern of work fits in well with children at school as you do not have to work during the holidays. Like part-time work it enables you to gain different experiences. This sort of work is available in many different professions such as offices, nursing and teaching. You will have to be prepared not to have a regular income and possibly to be called for work at very short notice. You may not be able to plan in advance. Many temporary workers find that employers eventually ask for them by name, even if they were originally part of a 'pool' or from an agency so that they do become familiar with their workplace and its systems. As with part-time work some temps have a greater chance of achieving a permanent or regular position with their employers, having been on the spot when vacancies arose.

Freelancing

Freelancers are self-employed people who offer their services to many different companies. This gives them the flexibility to work from home when it most suits them. It is important to study the conditions of self-employment. If you are keen to freelance, read the chapter in this book concerned with working for yourself.

Flexibility

When considering a different working pattern you will need to use initiative to break away from the traditional ways of working. You will need to be inventive and find alternative solutions. You will be at a great advantage if you can identify in advance the needs of your prospective employer and then suggest, either in a letter or at an interview, how you might fit in.

9 Training and education

The first thing that anyone considering undertaking any form of training or education will realize is that it is difficult to find a central, comprehensive authority dealing with what is available and where to find it. Don't let this put you off as there are in fact so many types of courses available that, in most cases, you can choose what best fits in to your lifestyle. You will have to consider the research needed to make your choice as a first step to the discipline of returning to study.

Bernadette had started teacher training when she left school but had given up to follow a career in retailing which came to an end when her two children were born. When they started school she became increasingly interested in returning to her first career choice. However, she was definite that she wanted a part-time course which would fit in with her two small children.

Not knowing where to look first she went to her local library but found that the prospectuses available were not comprehensive and were often out of date. She then started to ring various colleges in the locality who sent up-to-date prospectuses but were unable to advise her as to whether other colleges ran part-time teacher training courses.

THERE ARE MANY TYPES OF COURSES AVAILABLE . . . .

'It was very long-winded and I did feel like giving up. I must have made at least 20 phone calls, people passing me on to another number. There seemed to be no central body that could give me the information I needed.'

Eventually she contacted the education department at her county hall but even they could not provide her with the information she needed. However they did advise her to contact the Department of Education and Science who were immediately able to help her with courses in this area.

Now Bernadette must decide whether in fact part-time training is really the answer. Due to the travelling needed to reach the college where a suitable part time course takes place, she will still need to make arrangements for the children to be collected and looked after when school ends.

Where to find information

For the person who is not quite sure what they want to do, the library and job centre are the first places to visit as they will give an indication of the types of courses available and addresses where further information can be obtained. An excellent book which gives guidance on the types of training available and help with making your choice and is full of useful addresses is: *Second Chances – The guide to adult education and training opportunities*, a yearbook by Andrew Pates and Martin Good (Great Ouse Press).

Use your library well; the librarian will be able to tell you where to find information and if a book is not immediately available it may be ordered. There are directories giving addresses of various advice bodies such as the Council for National Academic Awards (CNAA), the Department of Education and Science and the Scottish Education Department, who also give guidance on grants available. The addresses of these organizations are listed at the back of the book.

There are compendiums of adult education courses such as *The Yearbook of Adult Education*, compiled by the National Institute of Adult Education which details local colleges, polytechnics and universities.

From the library you can obtain addresses of professional institutes. These should certainly be contacted if you are interested in a specific area as they will usually be able to give you careers advice. Some libraries also carry copies of specialist publications which give details of related courses. Specialist journals also carry job adverts which give you some indication of the levels of qualifications required by different jobs.

Job centres are also training centres. Not everyone realizes that its staff are on hand to advise on government-run training schemes. These are funded by the Manpower Services Commission and cover all aspects of training for employment, including refresher courses, how to write curriculum vitae and apply for jobs. There are also more specialized courses for which a training allowance is payable, and the venue is as varied as the subject matter. One course might take place in a local College of Further Education while another venue might be a local hall. Staff will not necessarily be able to give you a complete detailed list of what is available and where however, but will tell you who to contact for further information.

At the job centre you can also join the PER (Professional and Executive Recruitment) service. They publish a free newspaper, *Executive Post*, which carries details of developments in further education and training courses as well as courses currently available.

What is available?

'Leisure training'. Being at home is an ideal time to take the first step towards additional education by seeing it as a leisure pursuit. There are a huge variety of part-time courses that you can enrol in. These may not fit in with your ultimate career goal but will still increase your knowledge and skills, and are an ideal way of trying out subjects for the first time. They can then be studied more fully if desired.

Local Authorities run adult education classes. Prospectuses can be found in your library.

The Workers' Educational Association run short part-time courses on many different subjects during the day or evening and daytime courses usually have child care facilities. If you feel unable to join a class remember that reading is in itself an education. Pick a subject that you think might interest you and start with the books in your local library or bookshop. Move on to visiting specialist libraries in institutions and subscribe to magazines produced by professional bodies or interest groups, e.g. *National Geographic* magazine.

Training workshops

We have already mentioned government-run training schemes but there are others, too. Women's groups, apart from having classes, talks and discussions on women's issues, run courses on increasing self-confidence, opportunities for women, and provide mutual support. Many of these have creches while courses are running. To find your local women's group ask at your local Citizens' Advice Bureau or library and keep an eye on the women's pages of your local paper. Here, too, you may find courses of this type advertised or contact the Women's National Commission.

You may be lucky enough to have a local women's training and education group like the Newham Association for the Education and Training of Women, but if you don't there are some national networks that might help such as The Women Returners' Network, who have also compiled an invaluable directory of courses available throughout the country. Published by Longman it is called *Returning to Work*.

Other helpful networks are the Women and Training Group who have regional groups and provide details of local courses and produce a quarterly newsletter with all sorts of training news. Women in Management, a voluntary organization particularly concerned with management career opportunities for women and the Women's Engineering Society, who promote the study and practice of engineering among women, can both help women who wish to break into these particular career areas.

The Industrial Society run various developmental courses and its Pepperell unit is concerned with opportunities for women including, assertion training and career and management development skills for women.

If you have been interested in community and voluntary work, 'Interchange' is an agency which provides various services, including courses on management training and training related to this sort of work.

Gaining qualifications

You may need some formal qualifications to follow your chosen career plan, or you may need to gain extra ones. There are a variety of ways in which you can achieve this. As a 'mature student' you may be able to step into education higher up the ladder without 'O' and 'A' levels, so don't let the lack of them stop you.

The type of course you choose will depend on your situation. There are those that you can work on from home but before you decide you will have to consider whether you are able to study on your own on a regular basis and you should look carefully at what learning resources you will be using, whether radio and TV, cassettes or solely books. You will also have to consider how your assignments are marked and whether you need access to college facilities like science laboratories. You will need to work out how much time a week you must spend studying.

THERE ARE THOSE THAT YOU CAN WORK ON FROM HOME....

If you decide to work at home you can consider an Open University course which has the advantage of being very flexible in the length of time taken to achieve your goal, in the entry qualifications and in the fields of interest. You can follow a wide choice of topics of personal interest without commiting yourself to a final qualification, although these do count if you decide at a later stage to achieve that aim.

Correspondence courses are another form of home study. Large colleges offering such courses advertise in the national press or contact the Council of Accreditation of Correspondence Colleges for a list which will include courses of a specific occupational nature.

'Flexistudy' is the trade name of a learning system owned by the National Extension College, which combines home study with the use of local college resources and the support of tutors at that college. The NEC also publish an *Open Tech Directory* which includes a wide range of courses in all subjects for study at home.

If you would prefer to work with the encouragement and support of other pupils and a tutor, or if you find home learning too expensive, you can consider the more traditional places of study. Higher education and further education colleges, polytechnics and universities all offer courses leading to formal qualifications. It is important to choose the type of college and qualification carefully, bearing in mind the eventual outcome in relation to your career goal. You may like to contact an advisory body such as the Advisory Council For Adult and Continuing Education for information and advice or refer to the *Second Chances* book mentioned earlier.

If you are not sure whether you are ready to go on to studying, consider taking an access course. This is a preparation course for higher education designed for people with few formal qualifications. Nine out of ten people who complete the course do in fact go on to higher education.

Why you should consider education and training

Training is an investment in your earning potential and will help your career to develop whether or not it entails gaining formal qualifications. You can use it to learn new skills, develop interests or update current skills. It gives you something to offer employers and shows that you are capable of commitment. It will also help your personal development. It will broaden your outlook, help you gain new ideas and experiences and increase your confidence. It is very likely that it will lead on to other avenues and will certainly improve your promotion prospects. Quite apart from this you will probably enjoy the training and will meet new people.

Val had been a court clerk before her children were born. As they grew up she realized that she couldn't go back. It had to be a full-time occupation and she wasn't ready for that yet. She decided to update her secretarial skills by attending a government-sponsored typing and shorthand refresher course also involving learning to use a computer and word processor keyboard. The 12–week course took place at a nearby college and fitted in with her youngest son's hours at a nursery school. During her last week at the college she saw an internal 10-hour secretarial post advertised which she applied for and got. It involved working for the head of business studies, arranging the same kind of adult and youth training schemes as the one she had just completed. The pay was low and she put in many extra hours, however when her contract ended, her official hours were increased, until by the time her son started school she was working for three days a week.

She then embarked on a two-year part-time City and Guilds information technology course to gain a qualification to enable her to teach adults. While still on this course she was offered a job teaching the use of the word processor. She felt that if she didn't grasp this opportunity it might not be offered again so she took computer manuals home and relied on the support of her tutor.

The first time she faced a class she was so scared that she felt sick and was shaking inside but she appeared confident and had planned her lesson extremely well. She was given more hours to teach until she was taken on as a part-time tutor working 9 a.m. to 3 p.m. with just the odd evening work. She has had to give up the secretarial work as she has started a new career. For the future she is considering studying law, again concentrating on one aspect of the law, for instance licensing laws. Who knows where this course of study will lead?

10 Working for yourself

WOMEN ARE FINDING THERE ARE MANY ATTRACTIONS TO BEING THEIR OWN BOSS....

Women can work for themselves and more than ever are choosing to do so. Since the beginning of the 1980s the number of self-employed men rose by two per cent whilst the number of self-employed women rose by 24 per cent. Women are finding that there are many attractions to being their own boss, especially when they have got used to running their own show during a spell at home full-time.

Why work for yourself?

One of the great advantages of working for yourself is the opportunity to set your own hours and make use of the skills and resources that you have built up as part of home management. Married women may already benefit from having a regular income earned by husbands to reduce the financial risk but also single women with children have found their own business an ideal way to support the family whilst being around to care for their needs.

Chris bought a small secretarial agency from her share of the sale of her house when she separated from her husband. Living on the premises enabled her to care for her daughter whilst running the business. Jackie was already involved in direct sales of cosmetics when she got divorced so she was able to develop and improve her business to maintain a good income to keep her family.

One of the main reasons women choose to work for themselves is the desire to be independent from the inflexible hours of a job, from office politics and, in many areas, the lack of opportunity for challenging, interesting and varied work with prospects. Women recognize there is life beyond work and having tested this during a career break are reluctant to sacrifice freedom to return to work which is separated from the home and local community. Working for yourself can offer more chances to keep control over your lifestyle as well as fulfilling the need to develop skills and earn money.

WOMEN RECOGNIZE THERE IS LIFE BEYOND WORK....

How do women start in business?

A woman's approach to starting a business is quite often different to a man's, although the basic rules of business still apply. Because women often have a different starting point and separate experiences to men, they are more likely to view working for themselves with a more flexible attitude. Already working from home as a home manager and usually doing most of the shopping, women are more in touch with the local community and are able to spot gaps in demand or services. Their regular contact with other women at home provides a source of ideas and customers that can form the basis of a business idea.

Marilyn saw that a lot of women she met found difficulty in shedding unwanted weight so she set about forming a slimming club using a special health product. She was able to charge for membership of the club, make a profit on the slimming product and introduce her members to other health products that she sold, thus expanding her business. Now she is planning to extend her clubs to other parts of the country.

Christine was asked to keep an eye on a neighbour's house which was left empty for a while because it didn't sell. This gave her the idea to offer her services to people on the move, cleaning the house when the removal men had left and arranging supply services for people moving into a new house. She developed the business by approaching local firms with employees on the move as well as estate agents and building companies. The service was extended to offer decorating and information on local amenities for people new to the area – and with great success.

Help for putting your ideas into action

Ideas are one thing but putting them into action is another. Although women have many of the practical skills for running a business, like being able to cope with several things at once (essential skill for child rearing!), they often lack the confidence to get started. If you have never had any experience of business it can seem a very daunting prospect with hurdles like bank managers, VAT, tax, marketing, etc., to contend with. If you feel lack of 'know how' is your greatest obstacle then go down to your nearest job centre and ask about business training courses run locally. Find out where your nearest Enterprise Agency is situated and make an appointment to see a consultant for free advice. Put your ideas on paper so he or she can get a clear idea of what your intentions are.

The range of business training available is wide and varied with courses run at local colleges and polytechnics as well as workshops sponsored by the Manpower Services Commission. The Open University also runs a course for those wishing to start up a business and the library should carry details of these and any other business correspondence courses as well as books and tapes offering advice.

There are an increasing number of courses designed especially for women and these are an excellent starting point because they take into account the special needs of women, including child care needs and self-assertion. One of the best aspects of these courses is the opportunity they present to meet other enterprising women to share ideas and experiences. If you are starting alone you will find the contacts you make a real morale booster.

Find out if you have what it takes

Business training has been proved to increase your chances of success enormously, though it is still not a substitute for the hard work and dedication which are the main ingredients of achievement. Most women who have had families are used to hard work and are unlikely to be daunted by the prospect but it is still important to be sure you have the perseverence to succeed. Look back at the personality traits questionnaire that you filled in on page 21 and identify the qualities you have that will help you become a businesswoman. Are you intuitive? Can you spot connections and capitalize on the opportunities around you? Are you persistent and capable of seeing an idea through? Are you industrious and creative enough to develop your ideas? Are you well organized and self-motivated? Are you able to make time and space for your ideas? Don't be too dismayed if you feel you have failings – business skills can be developed in the same way as any other skills so long as you are truly motivated to make a go of it.

The most common way for women to start their own business is to choose an idea that can be run from home. There are a wide range of options open and your choice will be determined by your skills, i.e. training or experience, or your resources, for instance space, money and equipment, and the market, which in most cases will be local.

Professional services

Many of the skills which were developed through work can be sold from home as a freelance service or consultancy.

Eva worked with a PR agency before the birth of her son, who proved to be a difficult baby to cope with. Rather than go back to a full-time job she converted her loft into an office and began working from home doing public relations for a local company. She now has a range of clients, including a major PR agency, and can pay for a nanny to come in and look after her son and new baby daughter while she retreats to her office.

The variety of skills that can be sold in this way range from hairdressing, translations, home tutoring, to interior design consultancy, journalism and market research. All that is usually needed are the basic tools of the trade: a desk, filing cabinet, telephone with answering machine, word processor if possible, typewriter and a good set of headed stationery. Many companies find it more efficient to buy in services as and when they need them rather than to employ regular staff, so have the courage to go out and sell yourself. Look smart and be smart, you have nothing to lose and everything to gain.

Home production

Producing things at home is part of most women's everyday experience, whether cooking, knitting, crafts, dressmaking or making a garden grow. If you are particularly skilled at making something then there is a good chance others less skilled will be prepared to buy it.

Carol's speciality was homemade pizza so she took some samples to the local bakery and supermarket. They liked it and so did their customers and it was the start of a successful business.

Louise and Suzy were imaginative as well as good at sewing and they developed designer bibs for babies. They were so successful that their product was selected by the design centre and they increased production to over 120 bibs a week and had more than 24 outlets nationwide. There is a good market for speciality products at present and it is open to women with simple but clever ideas to exploit.

Making things from home will depend on the space and equipment you have available and you must be careful to check the rules governing certain types of production, like using industrial sewing machines which can cause noise nuisance. You can find out about this by contacting your local civic centre or get advice from your local Enterprise Agency. There are also strict rules governing the production of food to sell so be careful to check on hygiene, packaging and health and safety rules. You can refer to *Croner's reference book for self-employed and smaller business,* which you should be able to obtain at your local library. An excellent book to get hold of, covering all aspects of this subject, is *Home cooking for money* by Julia Ridgway (Book Club Associates, 1983).

If you have already got an expensive piece of equipment like a word processor or knitting machine then make it work for you.

Marjorie bought a typewriter to type her husband's thesis, saving him expensive typing charges, and then offered her services to other students. This paid for the machine and gave her extra income.

Word processors now offer the opportunity to make this kind of work easier and more effective and can be purchased at a very reasonable cost.

Maria invested in a word processor and then approached some local companies offering a variety of services from personalized letters, listings, circulars, reports to processing accounts. She found a positive response leading to a successful business. As her confidence grew, Maria bought computer magazines and learned to write programmes on the computer and could extend her services to offering customized programming for companies.

There are several books on the subject of working from home with useful information, ideas and advice. It is a growing industry because women in particular are increasingly finding it an ideal way of earning extra cash in their own time and space. There are a growing number of business networks or clubs designed to help people working from home.

Janet was a civil servant until the birth of her son when she felt she would miss out on too much of his development if she continued to work full-time. She felt there were likely to be many other women like herself who wanted to work as well as care for young children. She decided to set up a network which would bring women with skills together and act as an agent to sell their skills to local businesses, allowing them to work from home. She contacted her local paper and told them about her ideas and set a date for a meeting. The reporter did a small feature which brought a good response from women wanting to join the network. The Harrow Business Network is now a flourishing enterprise with a wide range of clients, providing work for a growing number of network members who are trained to the agency's standards.

Combine your skills – work with others

One of the advantages of working with an agency or a network is the contact it brings with other working people. You may be the kind of person who would find working alone difficult because of isolation or lack of motivation to get on with things. Partnerships are one way to get round this and can provide other benefits like sharing childcare and other responsibilities, complementing skills and adding to your resources. Partnerships are one of the closest relationships to marriage so be sure you find someone you are not only compatible with but someone with whom you have mutual trust and respect. It is wise to have a partnership agreement right from the start so there is no misunderstanding about money, responsibilities and policy as well as how to separate if you choose to leave the business at a later stage. The Partnership Act, 1949, covers many of these aspects so it is worth getting a book from the library to give guidance and consulting a solicitor for advice. You can, however, write your own agreement using these guidelines.

Co-operatives are also a growing industry and are suitable for any business that can be run by a team of people. Registered co-ops must have at least seven members who share the running and profits of the business. It can be a new venture or, in some cases, a way of taking over an existing business. It must have a democratic constitution which enables members to vote on important decisions and be able to compete with other types of business. The advantage of a co-operative, like a partnership, is the increased resources created by a spread of knowledge and capital as well as shared risk. ICOM (Industrial Common Ownership Movement), will provide advice and information on all aspects of running a co-op and they also run women's link-up courses in 10 local areas so it is worth finding out if there is one near you.

Another increasingly popular way to start a business with assistance is to run a franchise. This means that you pay a lump sum of money plus a percentage of your turnover, usually between five and ten per cent in return for all the back-up of a large organization. This may include training, market research, company image, an established product and marketing techniques. There is a very wide and growing range of businesses to choose from, some of which may already be familiar, like Wimpy restaurants, Tie Rack, Poppies. If you have the ability to raise a lump sum

CO-OPERATIVES ARE SUITABLE FOR ANY BUSINESS THAT CAN BE RUN BY A TEAM....

of money, (banks are usually willing to lend up to 70 per cent of the total sum required as against only 50 per cent for other types of business ventures), you may find this the ideal way to run your own show without all the headaches of learning by your mistakes.

Direct selling

The cost of purchasing a franchise, which may run into several thousands of pounds, may be too high in terms of commitments as well as money. It is possible to build a business with similar advantages to franchising, like an established product and company back-up, at a very much smaller outlay by becoming involved in direct sales or selling from home. This type of business is well known by anyone who has attended a Tupperware party or had the Avon lady calling. Products are sold by individuals operating through their network of friends and contacts, either by visiting them in their own homes or inviting them to a selling party or demonstration.

There are many products available from direct selling companies including jewellery, pottery, health and beauty products, clothes and so on, which are in different price ranges according to choice. This type of business can be an excellent starting point for women to learn business and marketing skills whilst at home, and at the same time earn some extra cash. Training is often given by established sales people and the initial money needed to get started can be as low as you like and with some companies you can pay as you sell.

Selling policies and ways of operating differ with each company so it is a good idea to investigate one or two of your choice before committing yourself to training and to purchasing stock. The Direct Selling Association, based at 44 Russell Square, London WC1, can give you a list of their member organizations if you send a stamped, addressed envelope.

Direct selling, like any other business, depends upon your determination to have a go and keep working at it until you start to see results. You have to be prepared to invest time and money in order to build up your business and there are no short cuts to establishing a good reputation by giving excellent service and value. Whether you start by using your spare room to run a bed and breakfast service or convert your house into a hotel, you must start with a business plan which contains details of the how, when, where and why of your business idea. You will need to think about the costs involved and plan out how you hope to get back these costs and make a profit. Guidelines on all the basic preparations for starting a business are available in a wide range of books (see particularly *The woman's guide to starting your own business*, published by Thorsons, 1988) and magazines so it is worth doing your homework first. Once you have started working on your business plan

BE PREPARED TO REVIEW YOUR IDEAS REGULARLY....

you must be prepared to review your ideas regularly, checking that your prices are right, that the quality is up to standard and that you are getting enough publicity. Your plan should show alternative or additional activities you could develop to expand or cope with slack times and should include targets or goals for you to reach to keep a check on whether you are on the right road.

Working for yourself can be exciting and rewarding because of the potential it offers for self development and self-fulfilment. For women, like Anita Roddick of the Body Shop, it brought success beyond her wildest dreams but for most women it brings the chance to prove themselves and the satisfaction of knowing they did it alone.

11 Public life

Women can and should take part in public life where decisions are taken that affect our lives in many ways. Public appointments range from local parish councils to government committees influencing the practice and running of all aspects of society, as varied as care in the local community or nuclear power policies. At present women have very little say in public life as they occupy only 11 per cent of general appointments and a much smaller proportion of higher-paid appointments – a poor showing for over half the nation's population.

Why are there so few women?

One of the problems for women has been their failure to put themselves forward for appointments, whether through politics, the media or public service generally. Women have been used to taking a back seat and encouraged to make the tea and support their husbands rather than consider taking a front-line role. The general lack of experience and confidence this has led to amongst women has caused men to say there are not enough suitable women available to take public appointments, so men continue to get the jobs. This is, of course, a vicious circle which can only be broken by women getting involved and gaining the experience necessary to get recognition.

Where does public life begin?

The best place to start learning about public life is right on your doorstep in the local community. If you have no experience at all of working with public bodies then begin by taking part in a local committee and becoming active in its work. Read the local papers carefully and identify what groups are active and what issues are of local concern. Take note of the groups and individuals who are getting good press coverage, especially the campaigns in operation which may be controversial but eyecatching. Choose a group or cause that you feel you have some commitment to. Decide how much time and effort you are willing and able to give and then attend all the meetings. Get to know all there is to know about them and offer your services.

How to get involved

Once you have pin-pointed a group you are interested in, find out who is the secretary. Details of voluntary groups can be found either in the local library, or the local council offices; through a local voluntary bureau or from the Citizens Advice Bureau. If it is a new campaign or group you have read about in the paper there will usually be a phone number and contact mentioned, if not phone the newspaper and ask for these details. Get the name of the secretary and phone him or her to ask for more details about the organization. Say you are interested in joining and find out when the next meeting will be held so that you can attend. Most groups are delighted to have new members and will be very welcoming, so don't hesitate to make the call. You are bound to feel nervous about going to the first meeting, especially if you don't know anyone involved, but remember – everyone was a new member once.

Your first meeting

If you have never attended a committee meeting before you may find it confusing to follow what is going on – especially if it is held in quite a formal manner. There are general rules to follow which ensure that the meeting is run efficiently; that everyone present gets a chance to speak if they wish and that notes are taken on what happens at the meeting. These are known as procedures, which are easy to follow once they are known and understood. Meetings usually have office holders present: a chairperson to run the meeting and keep everyone in order; a secretary to take notes (or minutes as they are known in formal terms) and a treasurer to report on the money involved in running the group.

Other posts are held according to the needs of the group, like a publicity officer or a membership secretary, otherwise interested people may just be committee members.

One way to help your confidence when attending a first meeting is to get a book from the library on meetings and read about procedures so you won't feel at a disadvantage when you attend. Of course you may find that the meeting is quite unbusinesslike in the way it is conducted in which case you will have the advantage!

Developing your skills

All positions in public life require confidence in the skills necessary. These can be developed by gaining experience as you go along but you must be prepared to take courage and have a go. By joining a committee you will gain experience of procedure and of following the committee style of working as a group to achieve a common aim. These are common to all kinds of meetings from the lowest level to the highest so once you have learned the basics you are ready for anything! Make sure you volunteer for jobs that stretch your talents; avoid making the tea and keeping backstage. Offer to take an official position that puts you in front, like publicity officer or fundraiser.

Public speaking is an important part of public life but however nervous you are at the thought of standing up in front of an audience, you will be surprised by how quickly you can develop this confidence once you get started. You can start by simply standing up and making a statement or asking a question at a general meeting – the first time is always the worst – and don't be afraid to speak out. Make your point short, loud and clear, and have the facts to back it up. If you have done your homework and know what you are talking about you can't go wrong.

Becoming an expert or an authority on a subject is a good qualification for public life. This is usually built up over a period of time by working in a special area and gaining a reputation for being able to speak on a subject.

Joan's first taste of public meetings was through the Women's Institute, where she learned the ropes of committee meetings. She felt passionately about the need for women to have more say in political life and so joined the 300 Group and helped run local meetings. This quickly developed to a position on the local parish council where she could voice her views on health care for women, amongst other issues that affected women's lives. She soon found she was being asked by the local papers to comment on these issues, which led to local people asking for help with campaigns concerning the local community. As her experience and reputation grew she eventually found herself being asked to sit on a national committee as the Welsh representative and now travels all over the country attending meetings and conferences.

Becoming an authority on a subject can start from a very personal concern. If you are involved in an area where there is a gap in services or understanding you may soon find that opportunities present themselves to make your voice heard by approaching newspapers, magazines and other public bodies. To do this effectively you must learn to communicate your information clearly and with facts to back it up. If you can speak well and make an impression you may find further interest is stirred and get more offers to speak or write publicly.

Be ambitious about your aims

If you want to make progress and improve your chances of getting a government appointment then you must work out a strategy to achieve this in the same way that you would if working for a large company. The same rules apply about looking ahead and planning your moves to create opportunities for yourself. As we said at the beginning, women don't get public appointments partly because they don't put themselves forward, so find ways to get noticed. Follow news items and issues of concern and be prepared to phone in or write about them wherever they appear. How you do this will depend on your areas of interest, whether political or otherwise. You may start at the bottom but make sure you don't stay there. Be prepared to move from a branch committee to a central committee, from a local campaign to a national campaign, from borough interests to regional interests.

Get help with your aims

You should be able to get a great deal of help from the organization you belong to through the information they produce and the individuals who are already successfully involved in them. There are other networks which can also give you help and two of the most important for women wanting to enter public life are:

The Women Into Public Life Campaign, which was formed to put pressure on governments to make more public appointments available to women. The campaign started by compiling a list of 500 curriculum

LEARN TO COMMUNICATE EFFECTIVELY....

vitae of women who are suitably qualified to take a public appointment. This was presented to the government minister to counter the argument that they don't have enough suitable women candidates. The campaign was supported by a wide range of well-known women and helped by the Women's National Commission which published an information booklet of government appointments called *Women into Public Appointments*. The Women into Public Life Campaign now has a part time co-ordinator, funded by the Equal Opportunities Commission and can be reached at the headquarters of the 300 Group.

The 300 Group is a women's network set up to help and encourage women to enter political life at all levels. The title '300 Group' was chosen because this is the number of women needed to become MPs if equal representation is ever to be achieved in parliament. The headquarters are in London but there are many local groups operating around the country, running meetings, talks and workshops. It is an all-party organization and should be supported by all women who have an interest in politics.

Many of the positions in public life are unpaid, including some of the government appointments, so you must think carefully about the expenses that may be involved. Even local councillors don't get paid for the many long hours they put in, although they do get expenses for attendance. If you work with a campaign, charity or political party you may not even get expenses. The reward from this type of work comes from the feeling of involvement, the chance to influence events and the opportunity for self-fulfilment by learning new skills and gaining new friends. Once you have gained good skills and experience you will be in a position to write a good CV and put your name forward to the cabinet office to be available for a public appointment, for which you may be paid. With the growing awareness of a need for greater equality for women, now is a good time to start.

A survey of some relevant courses

Address	Course title	Subjects covered	Notes
Thurrock Technical College, Woodview, Grays, Essex RM16 4YR.	Diploma in Play Leadership	Physical and emotional development of children; theories of play; influence of society on child; role of play worker.	1 year full-time £55.70 Creche facilities available. Course includes practical experience. No formal qualifications needed. Experience working with children.

The only full-time course in play leadership in the country. However there are a large number of part-time local courses. For further information contact: Shirley Toull, National Playing Fields Association, 25 Ovington Square, London SW3 1LQ. For information on short courses contact: Rocky Sharrock, Playtech, The Play Co-operative Ltd, Zair Works, 111–119 Bishop Street, Birmingham B5 6JL.

Address	Course title	Subjects covered	Notes
Bradford and Ilkley Community College, Wells Road, Ilkley, W. Yorks LS29 9RD	Certificate in Youth and Community Work	Human development; counselling; group work; youth and community service; welfare rights; influence of class, gender, race; community leisure; education; religion; deviance.	2 years full-time. No fee. 5 O levels usually required. This may be waived for mature students with some experience of working with people.

Many similar full-time and part-time courses available. For details of full-time and degree level courses contact: Council for Education and Training in Youth and Community Work, Wellington House, Wellington Street, Leicester LE1 6HL. Their *Initial Training* booklet costs £1 + p&p.

Address	Course title	Subjects covered	Notes
Henley Management College, Greenlands, Henley-on-Thames, Oxon RG9 3AU	The New Henley Management Course	Management skills; accounting; operations and logistics; data processing; personnel; interviewing and appraisal; investment analysis; marketing; purchasing; public speaking and presentation; organizational structures; corporate leadership; communication; negotiation plus a personal learning package drawn up to meet individual needs and interests.	6 months – 2 years. The course is built around four core modules taken at the college. The remainder is by distance learning. Can lead to Henley Management Diploma or Master of Business Administration (MBA) degree. £4,400 + VAT. Intended for those with experience of middle management. Bursaries available.
Hatfield Polytechnic, School of Business and Social Sciences, Mangrove Road, Hertford ST13 8QF	Diploma of Management Studies	Finance; economics; organizational behaviour; law; personal skills; time management; assertiveness; interviewing; design of a business game. Plus an electric in-depth topic; and a work-based project.	1 year full-time. Course arranged to fit around school hours. Degree or managerial experience necessary. £1,100 discretionary LEA grants available. High success rate for women getting jobs at end of course. For further details write to course tutor, Iris Smith.

Address	Course title	Subjects covered	Notes
Hatfield Polytechnic (address as above)	Accountancy foundation course	Financial and management accounting; economics; law; business and society; quantitative methods; business computing.	1 year full-time 10 a.m.–3 p.m. Relevant experience or 2 A levels (grade C+). Aptitude for maths. £556. LEA discretionary grant available. Course recognized by Association for Chartered Accountants. Many women go on to join accountancy firms and take further training.
Sheffield Women's Technology Training Workshop, Thomas Street, Sheffield S. Yorks S1 4LE	Electronics and Computing. Certificate in Information Technology and Electronics (City & Guilds) optional.	Electronics; computing; maths general studies; return to work.	1 year part-time (15 hours a week). No qualifications needed. Free. £16 expenses allowance paid to students. Opportunities to enter further or higher education in management, computing, information technology, or to get jobs.

Similar women's training workshops in larger cities. Contact your local council information department to see if there is one near you.

Address	Course title	Subjects covered	Notes
Mid Wales Development, Ladywell House, Newtown, Powys SY16 1JB	Getting into business	Self-employment; personal skills and qualities; prices and product costing; business plan; sources of money; cash flow; VAT; market research; time management; bookkeeping; how to use an accountant; insurance.	2 months part-time. Introductory course for those wanting to set up their own business. Content flexible according to needs. Held at various venues throughout mid Wales. Free. MSC backed.
Manpower Services Commission, Government Buildings, Gladstone Road, Northampton NN5 7QA	Northamptonshire Private Enterprise Programme	Marketing techniques; selling; sales promotions. Finance: control; bookkeeping; accounting; finding finance; computerized accounting. Management: development product range; employing others; computers; managing growth.	To help those already running small businesses. Course organized in modules. You can either enrol for whole module, or attend individual seminars at various centres in area. £35 per seminar or £210 per module (maximum).

These are just two of the MSC courses designed to help small businesses. For similar courses in your area contact the Job Centre, or local authority Enterprise Agency.

Address	Course title	Subjects covered	Notes
Engineering Employers Association of the West Midlands, St James House, Frederick Road, Edgbaston, Birmingham B15 1JJ	Women in Management	Finance; marketing; production; personnel management; communication skills; plus a four-week management project in a local company.	12 weeks full-time. You need either some experience of management, or qualifications but no experience. Mixed ability groups. Age range between 22 and 50. Free. MSC backed. Training allowance of £38 a week is payable. 85% of those completing course get jobs in management. Contact course tutor Juanita Cockton.
Industrial Society, Robert Hyde House, 48 Bryanton Square, London W1H 7LN	Change your career	Possible new directions; evaluating your skills; making the most of opportunities; action plan.	One day. No qualifications needed. £40 + VAT. The society also runs other courses for women. Contact Fiona Cannon.

Address	Course title	Subjects covered	Notes
Hillcroft College, South Bank, Surbiton, Surrey KT6 6DF	CNAA Certificate in Combined or Social Studies	Wide range of subjects in the humanities, including sociology, social policy, psychology. Social work placements — two days a week in first year; three in second.	1 to 2 years full-time. Recognized pre-entry to social work courses. No qualifications needed, but voluntary or paid experience in social work necessary. The college is mainly residential women-only. Some day places for those with family committments. £622 per year. Mandatory DES grant available.
Hillcroft College (address as above)	Wider Opportunities for Women	Career planning; assessment of previous learning; making choices; study skills; numeracy; range of courses in the humanities and social sciences.	Six weeks full-time 10 a.m. – 3 p.m. To prepare women for future work or higher education. No entry requirements. Free. MSC sponsored.

For Wider Opportunities courses in your area, ask at the Job Centre.

Address	Course title	Subjects covered	Notes
University of Southampton University Road, Highfield, Southampton	Second Chance for Women	A multi-disciplinary women's studies course specially for women who missed out on formal education.	10 weeks part-time, with the option of extending it by a further two terms. £24 a term. Bursaries available, and no woman should be deterred by lack of funds. In the past, course has been recognized for entry to higher education.

This is a short, selective survey of just a few courses on offer. The courses have been picked to show the wide rnage of cost, level and duration of training that is suited to the special needs of women. If you can't find the course you're after — keep looking. Enquire at your local college of further or higher education, ask for the organizer of adult or continuing education. Alternatively contact other educational establishments in your area, or for MSC courses the Job Centre. Keep an eye, too, on your local newspaper or library for details of classes. The opportunities are there if you are prepared to look for them.

Useful addresses

The Council for National Academic Awards (CNAA), 344–354 Gray's Inn Road, London WC1X 8BP

Department of Education and Science, Elizabeth House, York Road, London SE1 7PH

The Industrial Society, Peter Runge House, 3 Carlton House Terrace, London SW1Y 5DG

The 'Interchange' Trust, 15 Wilkin Street, London NW5 3NG

Manpower Services Commission: Check in the telephone directory for your local area office.

National Advisory Centre on Careers for Women (NACCW), 8th Floor, Artillery House, Artillery Row, London SW1P 1RT Tel: 01 380 0117

National Federation of Women's Institutes, 39 Eccleston Street, London SW1W 9NT
Tel: 01 730 7212

National Institute of Adult Education, De Montfort House, 196 De Montfort Street, Leicester LE1 76H

Newham Association for the Education and Training of Women, Memorial Baptist Church, 389 Barking Road, Plaiston, London E13 8AL

The Open University, PO Box 48, Milton Keynes MK7 6AA

The Pepperell Unit, Robert Hyde House, 48 Bryanston Square, London W1H 7LN

Scottish Education Department, Haymarket House, Clifton Terrace, Edinburgh EH12 5DT

Women and Manual Trades, c/o 52–54 Featherstone St, London EC1
Tel: 01 251 9192

The Women and Training Group GLOSCAT, Oxtalls Lane, Gloucester GL2 9HW

Women CAN, 32 The Mall, London N14 6LN

Women in Banking, c/o Beryl Bakewell, Bayerische Hypotheken und Wechsel Bank, Bucklersbury House, Queen Victoria Street, London EC4
Tel: 01 248 4252

Women in Management, 64 Marryat Road, Wimbledon, London SW19 5BN Tel: 01 946 1238

Women in Medicine, 7^{c} Cassland Road, London E9 Tel: 01 986 1275

Women into Management, 56 Charnwood Road, Shepshed, Leicestershire LE12 9NP

Women into Science, Engineering and Technology, 72 Highbury Park, London N5 2XE Tel: 01 354 2492

The Women Returners' Network, Ruth Michaels, Senior Tutor for Continuing Education, Hatfield Polytechnic, Hatfield

The Women's Engineering Society, Imperial College of Science and Technology, Department of Civil Engineering, Imperial College Road, London SW7 2BN

The Women's Film, TV and Video Network, 79 Wardour Street, London W1 Tel: 01 434 2076

The Women's National Commission, Government Offices, Great George Street, London SW1P 3AQ Tel: 01 270 5903

The Women's Register, 245 Warwick Road, Solihull, West Midlands B92 7AH Tel: 021 706 1101

The Workers Educational Association, Temple House, 9 Upper Berkeley Street, London W1H 8BY

The Working Mother's Association, 23 Webbs Road, London SW11 6RU Tel: 01 228 3757

Further reading

Jane Chapman, *Women working it out*, MSC/COIC, 1987.

COIC: *What can a nurse do?*; *What can a teach do except teach?*; *What else can a housewife do?*; *What else can a secretary do?* (Available from the Careers and Occupational Information Centre, Freepost, Sheffield S1 4BR.)

Ruth Miller and Anna Alston, *Equal Opportunities* (8th edition), Penguin, 1987.

Leslie Morphy, *Career Change: A new working direction*, Hobsons/CRAC, 1987.

Andrew Pates and Martin Good, *Second Chances: The guide to adult education and training opportunities*, Great Ouse Press (published annually).

Returning to Work: Education and training for women, Women Returners' Network/Longman 1987.

Glenna Sutcliffe, *Effective Learning for Effective Management*, Prentice Hall, 1988.

Index